INSPIRATIONAL BASKETBALL STORIES FOR KIDS

TERRIFIC TALES

ISBN: 978-1-915736-97-0 (Paperback)

ISBN: 978-1-915736-96-3 (Hardcover)

First printing edition 2024. Terrific Tales

admin@terrifictale.com

CONTENTS

To get all your exciting free bonuses, including extra trivia, fun facts, and quizzes, simply send an email to the address below. As soon as I receive your email, I'll send your bonus material right away!

Email: admin@terrifictale.com

INTRODUCTION

Welcome to a journey through the hardwood floors, the echoing dribbles, the swoosh of the nets, and the heart-pounding moments that define basketball. This is not just a book; it's an adventure into the world of basketball, seen through the eyes and lives of some of the most inspirational athletes who have ever graced the court. My love for basketball goes beyond just being a fan of the game; it's a passion that has shaped my life. It is this love and passion that I wish to share with you, in the hopes of igniting a similar fire in your heart.

I wrote this book with a simple aim: to get more kids interested in basketball and to encourage them to be active, both on and off the court. The lessons basketball teaches us about perseverance, teamwork, and determination are invaluable not just in sports, but in every part of life.

As you turn these pages, you'll encounter stories of legendary athletes who started just like you—dreaming big and facing challenges. You'll read about Michael Jordan's relentless pursuit of excellence that led him to become one of the greatest basketball players of all time, despite being cut from his high school basketball team. You'll learn about LeBron James, who rose from humble beginnings to dominate the world stage with his incredible talent and work ethic. And you'll be inspired by the story of Kobe Bryant, whose dedication and love for the game were evident in every move he made on the court.

But this book is not just about the legends. It's also about the unsung heroes of basketball, the incredible comebacks, and the moments that might not have made headlines but have left an unforgettable mark on the hearts of those who witnessed them. From awe-inspiring plays to acts of incredible sportsmanship, these stories showcase the true spirit of basketball.

Each chapter shows what can be achieved with hard work, belief, and a love for the game. Whether you're a seasoned player or just starting to explore the world of basketball, there's something in here for you. These stories are not just to be read; they're to be lived. As you dive headfirst into these tales, I hope you find inspiration, motivation, and the courage to chase your dreams, just as these athletes did.

So, lace up your sneakers and let's dive into the exhilarating world of basketball. Who knows? The next great story might just be yours.

CHAPTER 1
"MUGGSY" BOGUES

IN LIFE, YOU MIGHT FEEL OR BE TOLD THAT YOU ARE TOO small to do something. People will doubt your ability just because you're small in stature, but the next time someone mentions it, tell them about this story. Because in the land of giants that is the NBA, there was once a man named Muggsy Bogues who played in the league for 14 seasons and inspired a whole generation while only standing at 5 feet 3 inches. This is the incredible story of the little guy with a big heart.

TYRONE CURTIS
"MUGGSY"
BOGUES

In the heart of Baltimore, Maryland, a young boy named Tyrone Curtis "Muggsy" Bogues was about to embark on an incredible journey. Born on January 9, 1965, Muggsy grew up in the Lafayette Court housing projects, a place where dreams often died before they could even begin. Despite the challenges that surrounded him, Muggsy held onto a dream that seemed almost impossible for a boy who stood at just 5 feet 3 inches tall: to become a professional basketball player.

From the moment he first picked up a basketball, he was in love. The court became his home, a place where he could escape the troubles of the world around him. However, Muggsy quickly realized that his height—or lack of—made him an unlikely candidate for basketball stardom. But what he lacked in height, he made up for with his incredible speed, agility, and determination. Despite the skepticism he faced, Muggsy refused to let his dream die. He knew that to succeed, he would have to work harder than anyone else. Every morning before the sun rose, he was on the court, practicing his dribbling, shooting, and most importantly, learning how to outsmart players who towered over him.

Muggsy's hard work began to pay off during his time at Dunbar High School. Under the guidance of Coach Bob Wade, he became the heart and soul of what is considered one of the greatest high school basketball teams of all time.

His leadership and tenacity on the court inspired his team-mates to reach new heights, leading the team to an undefeated season and a national championship.

In Baltimore, Muggsy was a hero. His name echoed through the streets and gyms, synonymous with hard work and talent. Dunbar High had been his proving ground, where he show-cased that the heart of a champion beats louder than the roar of any crowd. Under the guidance of Coach Bob Wade, Muggsy had transformed from a young boy with a dream into a leader who inspired those around him. His senior year was a result of all the hard work, it shows that greatness comes in all sizes. Leading his team to an undefeated season and a national championship, he had done what many thought impossible. But as the final buzzer of his high school career sounded, a new challenge loomed on the horizon—college basketball.

The decision on where to continue his journey weighed heavily on Muggsy. Many colleges had shown interest, but few believed in him as much as Wake Forest University did. It was here that he would begin the next chapter of his journey. The criticism from outsiders was constant. "Too small for college ball," they said. "He'll be overshadowed by taller play-ers," others claimed. But Muggsy used the doubt as fuel, a relentless reminder of the barriers he was determined to break. His first season at Wake Forest was a revelation.

His speed, agility, and unmatched court vision made him an invaluable asset to the team. He wasn't just keeping up with the competition; he was outsmarting them, outplaying them, and, most importantly, outclassing them. His impact on the court was immediate and electrifying. He became known for his defensive prowess, often tasked with guarding the opposing team's best player. His ability to steal the ball and initiate the fast break became a hallmark of Wake Forest's gameplay. Muggsy was not only surviving in the world of college basketball; he was thriving.

After a standout college career at Wake Forest University, where he left as the school's all-time leader in assists and steals, Muggsy Bogues faced the next big challenge: the NBA Draft. In 1987, the Washington Bullets selected him with the 12th overall pick, a decision that would not only change his life but also send ripples through the basketball world. The draft was an important moment for Muggsy, proving to himself and the world that his basketball skill outweighs any limitations his size might suggest.

His rookie season with the Bullets was a period of adjustment, as it is for many first-year players. However, his speed, court vision, and tenacious defense quickly made him a standout player. Despite playing in only 79 games and starting in one, Muggsy made his presence felt on the court, showcasing his ability to compete at the highest level of basketball.

The real turning point in Muggsy's NBA career came when he was left unprotected by the Bullets in the 1988 expansion draft and was selected by the newly formed Charlotte Hornets. In

Charlotte, he found not just a team but a home. He became the face of the franchise, beloved by fans for his heart, hustle, and sheer determination. His impact was immediate; he helped transform the Hornets from a fledgling expansion team into a competitive force in the NBA. Muggsy's leadership and energy were infectious, elevating the play of his teammates and turning the Hornets into a yearly playoff contender. His best season came in 1993-94 when he averaged 10.8 points, 10.1 assists, and 1.7 steals per game, showcasing his all-around skills and earning him widespread recognition.

For many, Muggsy's most memorable night came against the Cleveland Cavaliers. The game not only showcased his incredible skills on the court but also showed exactly what brought him so far in life: his heart and positive attitude.

On a crisp evening, with the arena lights shining down like stars in the night sky, a basketball game was set to unfold that would forever write itself into NBA history. This wasn't just any game; it was the Charlotte Hornets facing off against the Cleveland Cavaliers, a matchup that promised excitement. But more than that, it was a game that would showcase the incredible impact of Muggsy Bogues. Despite the endless chorus of doubters who said he was too small to play in the league, Muggsy had not only proved them wrong but had become an indispensable force for the Hornets. On this particular night, he was about to demonstrate why his stature was no measure of his greatness.

As the game tipped off, the energy in the arena was electric. Fans of all ages, some wearing Muggsy's jersey, watched eagerly as the players took to the court. From the outset, it was clear that Muggsy was in his groove. His speed and agility allowed him to weave through the Cavaliers' defense with ease, setting up his teammates for score after score. But his true impact was felt on defense. Despite his size, he was a tough opponent, stealing the ball from players nearly twice his height and sparking fast breaks that left the crowd in awe. The game was tightly contested, with both teams exchanging leads. However, as the final quarter began, Muggsy took control. With the Hornets trailing by a few points, he elevated his play to a level that seemed to inspire everyone around him. His defensive skill was on full display as he snatched the ball from a Cavaliers' player, darting down the court to score a crucial layup.

But he wasn't done yet. With the game hanging in the balance and the seconds ticking away, he showcased his incredible basketball IQ. Recognizing a double team on one of his taller teammates, Muggsy darted into the open space, received the pass, and, with a defender closing in, hit a jump shot that would have been a challenge for any player, let alone someone of his height.

The arena erupted into cheers as his shot went through the net. It was a moment of pure magic, a testament to the fact that heart and hustle can overcome any obstacle. The Cavaliers called a timeout, but the momentum had shifted. The Hornets, fueled by Muggsy's energy and leadership, tightened their defense and executed flawlessly on offense. In the final minutes, Muggsy continued to dazzle. He assisted on a key three-pointer, stole the ball in an important defensive stand, and managed the game's pace with the grace of a seasoned veteran. When the final buzzer sounded, the Hornets had secured a hard-fought victory, thanks in no small part to Muggsy's incredible performance.

As the fans left the arena, buzzing with excitement over what they had just witnessed, the story of the game was clear. Muggsy Bogues, the player many had doubted because of his height, had dominated the game in every way possible. His stat line was impressive, but it was his leadership, determination, and heart—that truly made the difference.

Despite his success, Muggsy's career was not without challenges. He faced constant criticism and was underestimated due to his height, with many doubting his ability to sustain a long career in a league dominated by much taller players. However, he used this as fuel, pushing himself harder and dedicating himself to proving his doubters wrong.

His resilience in the face of adversity was a hallmark of his career and served as an inspiration to many. After ten seasons with the Hornets, Muggsy went on to play for the Golden State Warriors and the Toronto Raptors before retiring. Throughout his 14-year NBA career, he defied the odds and left an unforgettable mark on the game of basketball. He finished his career with over 6,000 points, 6,000 assists, and 1,300 steals, solidifying his status as one of the most dynamic and impactful point guards in NBA history.

Beyond his statistical achievements, Muggsy's true legacy lies in the barriers he broke and the minds he changed. He demonstrated that success in basketball and in life is not predicated on physical attributes but on skill, determination, and heart. Muggsy Bogues remains an enduring figure of inspiration, not just for hopeful basketball players but for anyone facing seemingly impossible challenges *(Bogues, Tyrone "Muggsy" | Encyclopedia.com)*.

CAREER HIGHLIGTHS

- Muggsy was selected 12th overall by the Washington Bullets in the 1987 NBA Draft, making him the shortest player to ever be drafted in the first round.
- Muggsy is the all-time leader in assists and steals for the Charlotte Hornets, showcasing his playmaking ability and defensive prowess.
- Despite his primary role as a facilitator, Bogues was capable of scoring when needed, averaging double figures in points during several seasons.
- Known for his durability and toughness, Muggsy played in all 82 games in multiple NBA seasons.

- His size did not hold him back on defense. Instead, he used his low center of gravity and quickness to his advantage, often surprising opponents with his defensive capabilities.
- Muggsy Bogues inspired countless young athletes to pursue their dreams regardless of physical limitations. His story has been featured in documentaries, books, and motivational speeches across the globe.
- Holds the record for being the shortest player to ever play in the NBA. His career is often cited as a testament to skill, determination, and heart over physical limitations.

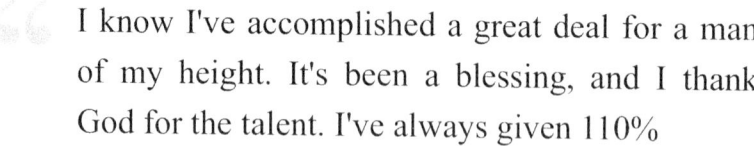

I know I've accomplished a great deal for a man of my height. It's been a blessing, and I thank God for the talent. I've always given 110%

Muggsy Bogues

CHAPTER 2
STEPH CURRY

ON THE NIGHT OF DECEMBER 14, 2021, HISTORY WAS MADE. The legend that is Steph Curry was about to ensure his name would be remembered in the NBA forever, by becoming the all-time leading three-point scorer. This not only symbolized his incredible skill but also highlighted the impact he has had on the NBA since he joined the league. Fittingly, the venue for such an important event was the famous Madison Square Garden arena in New York. Steph's Golden State Warriors were facing off against the Knicks, while the whole world held its breath, wondering if tonight would be the night Ray Allen's record of 2,973 three-pointers would be beaten.

Finally, the moment of triumph came in the early first quarter. Curry received the ball from Andrew Wiggins at the top of the key. In typical fashion, he released a quick 3-point shot over the defender's outstretched arm. And just like he had done so many times in his incredible career, he sent the ball sailing through the net, setting a new record of 2,974 three-pointers. The arena erupted into cheers, and the game was momentarily halted to celebrate this amazing achievement. Players, coaches, and celebrities in the venue all stood to congratulate this basketball legend. Ray Allen himself graciously passed the torch to Curry in a symbolic gesture of good respect between the two.

For many casual NBA fans, they might assume that Steph was always this basketball phenom, and his career must have started at the top and remained there. But they would be wrong. Even the legendary Steph Curry had been written off many times during his career. Scouts said he was too small in stature and lacked athleticism; they doubted his ability to compete with the big boys. Even when he made it to the league, he was plagued by injuries that threatened his career. But through all this doubt and bad luck, he remained positive and continued to work his socks off every day. Let's take a closer look at the life and career of the sharpshooting Steph Curry.

Wardell Stephen Curry II was born on March 14, 1988, in

Akron, Ohio, while his father, Dell Curry, was a member of the Cleveland Cavaliers.

Steph's journey from a lightly regarded high school player to an NBA superstar represents what perseverance, skill development, and the relentless pursuit of greatness can achieve. Growing up, Steph was immersed in the world of basketball from a very young age. His father, Dell, was a prolific sharpshooter himself, and the young Curry spent countless hours in NBA arenas, watching games and learning the ins and outs of the sport. Alongside his younger brother, Seth, Steph would engage in spirited games, practicing his skills from an early age. Despite his family background in basketball, his path to stardom was anything but assured.

As a child, Steph was undersized and often overlooked, not exhibiting the physical attributes that many coaches sought. However, what he lacked in size, he made up for with an incredible work ethic and a shooting touch that was evident even in his early years. Under the mentorship of his father, he developed a rigorous training plan, focusing on shooting, ballhandling, and basketball IQ.

His high school career began at Charlotte Christian School, where his slight frame and boyish appearance continued to cast doubts among observers about his potential at the next level.

Despite these challenges, Curry quickly established himself as a standout player, demonstrating an incredible ability to score from anywhere on the court. His senior year resulted in him averaging over 20 points per game, along with significant contributions in assists and steals, leading his team to conference championships and catching the attention of college scouts. However, the recruitment process was disheartening for Curry. Dreaming of playing for major Division I programs like his father, who had starred at Virginia Tech, Steph found himself largely ignored by top-tier schools. They cited concerns over his strength, athleticism, and defensive capabilities. The most significant snub came from his father's old college, which offered him a walk-on spot rather than a scholarship.

Davidson College, a small liberal arts school in North Carolina, became the unlikely stage for Steph's ascent. Under Coach Bob McKillop, Davidson offered Curry the scholarship and opportunity he sought to prove his doubters wrong. McKillop saw beyond the physical limitations, recognizing his exceptional shooting ability, basketball IQ, and potential for growth.

Curry's freshman season at Davidson was nothing short of spectacular. He announced his presence on the national stage by averaging 21.5 points per game, a remarkable feat that led all freshmen in scoring across the NCAA.

His ability to score from beyond the arc, coupled with his quick release and high basketball IQ, made him a nightmare for defenders. His season finished with him named the Southern Conference Freshman of the Year, setting the stage for even greater accomplishments.

The season witnessed Curry's evolution from a scoring freshman to a national sensation. He led Davidson on an unforgettable Cinderella run through the NCAA Tournament, reaching the Elite Eight. Along the way, his performances were nothing short of legendary, including a 40-point outburst against Gonzaga in the first round and leading his team past Georgetown and Wisconsin, both higher-seeded teams. By the end of the tournament, he had become a household name, praised for his scoring ability, leadership, and clutch performances. His sophomore season ended with him averaging 25.9 points per game and firmly established him as one of the nation's elite players.

In his junior year, Curry faced a new challenge as Coach McKillop shifted him from shooting guard to point guard, a move designed to prepare him for the NBA. This transition showcased his versatility and ability to adapt, as he not only continued to score at an elite level, averaging 28.6 points per game, but also led the nation in scoring and demonstrated improved passing and playmaking skills, averaging 5.6 assists per game.

Despite facing double teams and defenses aimed solely at containing him, Curry's performance never wavered. His stellar play led Davidson back to the NCAA Tournament, though they were unable to replicate the previous year's deep run. However, his individual achievements, including a myriad of school and conference records, solidified his status as one of college basketball's all-time greats.

After his junior year, Curry faced an important decision: return to Davidson for his senior year or declare for the NBA draft. After much thought, he announced his intention to enter the 2009 NBA Draft, leaving behind a collegiate legacy that was both inspiring and historic. His decision was met with mixed reactions; while his offensive skills were undeniable, many scouts questioned his ability to transition to the NBA due to his size and athleticism.

On June 25, 2009, the Golden State Warriors selected Stephen Curry with the seventh overall pick in the draft, a decision that would alter the franchise's destiny. The Warriors, interested in his shooting ability and potential to grow as a playmaker, took a chance on him despite the doubts about his physical attributes and defensive capabilities. Curry's transition to the NBA was not without its challenges. His rookie season was promising, as he averaged 17.5 points, 5.9 assists, and 4.5 rebounds per game, finishing second in the Rookie of the Year voting. Yet, his early years were plagued by ankle injuries, raising concerns about his long-term durability.

Despite these setbacks, Curry's work ethic and determination never wavered. He spent countless hours rehabilitating his ankles, refining his game, and gradually silencing the doubts that had followed him since high school.

The 2012-2013 season marked a turning point for Curry and the Warriors. Fully recovered from his ankle issues, he embarked on a campaign that would see him set a new NBA record for three-pointers made in a single season (272), a feat that shattered the previous mark and showcased his unparalleled shooting ability. His performance not only led the Warriors to their second playoff appearance in 19 years but also signaled the arrival of a new force in the league.

Curry's performances in the playoffs further solidified his status as an up-and-coming superstar. His ability to hit shots from seemingly impossible distances, often under intense pressure, excited fans and terrified opponents. The Warriors' upset of the Denver Nuggets in the first round, propelled by Curry's shooting, marked a significant moment in the team's rise and his own career.

His impact on the NBA extends far beyond his individual achievements. His success fundamentally altered how teams valued and utilized the three-point shot. Prior to his rise, the three-pointer was often seen as a secondary option. Curry, with his range and accuracy, demonstrated that it could be a primary weapon.

Teams across the league began to take note, and the strategic emphasis on three-point shooting increased dramatically. The Warriors, under the guidance of head coach Steve Kerr, embraced this philosophy fully, building a system around Curry's unique talents. This shift not only led to unprecedented success for the Warriors, including multiple championships but also influenced the tactical approaches of teams league-wide.

Stephen Curry's individual brilliance was a catalyst for the Golden State Warriors' transformation into a basketball giant. Under the coaching genius of Steve Kerr and alongside talented teammates like Klay Thompson, Draymond Green, and eventually Kevin Durant, Curry led a team that would redefine excellence in the NBA.

The Warriors' 2014-2015 season marked his first NBA Championship and Curry's first MVP award. Yet, it was the following season, 2015-2016, that the Warriors etched their name into the annals of history. Finishing the regular season with a record-breaking 73 wins, Golden State surpassed the 1995-1996 Chicago Bulls for the most victories in a single season. Curry was phenomenal, averaging 30.1 points per game and becoming the first unanimous MVP in league history, a feat that underscored his dominance and the respect he commanded across the sport.

Debates about the greatest team in NBA history are subjective and often influenced by peoples own opinions.

However, the Golden State Warriors, led by Curry during their peak years, certainly have a claim in this conversation. Their blend of shooting, defensive prowess, and unselfish ball movement revolutionized basketball, influencing how teams at all levels approach the game.

The Warriors' success was not just the result of assembling talented players but also a result of a team who believed in strength in numbers and the power of collective effort. Curry, with his influence on the court and selfless play, was the key to this approach, elevating the play of those around him and embodying the ethos that defined Golden State's dynasty.

Curry's journey from a doubted college prospect to the top of basketball achievement is a narrative of perseverance, innovation, and the relentless pursuit of greatness. By shattering the all-time three-point record and leading the Warriors to unparalleled success, he has not only secured his place in the pantheon of basketball greats but also transformed how the game is played and perceived.

Curry's impact is measured not only in the records he has set and the championships he has won but also in the countless young players who now step onto courts around the world, dreaming of emulating his success and shooting prowess.

In breaking the all-time three-point record and leading one of the greatest teams in NBA history, he has transcended the sport, becoming a symbol of excellence, innovation, and the infinite possibilities that lie beyond the arc. His story is an example of the power of belief, the beauty of the game, and the enduring legacy of a player who dared to be great (Biography.com Editors, 2024).

CAREER HIGHLIGHTS

- Curry has won multiple NBA championships with the Warriors, contributing significantly to the team's dynasty in the 2010s and early 2020s.
- He has won the NBA Most Valuable Player (MVP) award two times, including becoming the first unanimous MVP in league history during the 2015-2016 season.
- Curry has claimed several NBA scoring titles, showcasing his ability to score from anywhere on the court.
- He holds numerous NBA records for three-point shooting, including the records for most three-pointers made in a season and becoming the fastest player to reach 2,000 career three-pointers.
- He has represented the United States in international competition, winning gold medals at the FIBA World Championships and the Olympics.
- While Curry is still active and continues to build on his impressive career, he is widely regarded as a

future Hall of Famer for his on-court achievements and impact on the game.

 Success is not an accident, success is actually a choice.

STEPH CURRY

CHAPTER 3
DIRK NOWITZKI

IN THE QUAINT TOWN OF WÜRZBURG, GERMANY, OUR NEXT tale begins and sets the scene for one of the greatest underdog stories the NBA has ever known. Dirk Werner Nowitzki, born on June 19, 1978, was not just any child; he was a beacon of potential, destined to write his name in basketball history.

The turning point in Dirk's basketball journey came when Holger Geschwindner, a former German international player and a visionary basketball coach, spotted him. Recognizing Dirk's raw talent and untapped potential, Geschwindner took him under his wing, setting the stage for a mentorship that would change the course of his life. Dirk's dedication to improving his game paid off, and by the age of 16, he was dominating the local leagues, his name starting to spread across the basketball community in Germany. His performances caught the eye of the national team selectors, and soon, he was representing his country, showcasing his talent on an international stage.

Despite his rising star in Europe, Dirk's ambition was to test his mettle against the best in the world: the NBA. This dream seemed distant, given the relatively low profile of European players in the league at the time. However, his passion was unshakeable. In 1998, after a standout performance at the Nike Hoop Summit, where he dazzled scouts with his shooting ability and versatility against top American high school players, the path to the NBA began to form.

Skipping college basketball, a route traditionally taken by aspiring NBA players, he entered the 1998 NBA Draft. It was a bold move, full of uncertainty, but Dirk, backed by Geschwindner's unwavering support, was ready to take the leap. Selected ninth overall by the Milwaukee Bucks and immediately traded to the Dallas Mavericks, his NBA journey was about to begin.

The 1998-1999 NBA season, shortened due to a lockout, was a harsh introduction to professional basketball in the United States. He struggled with the physicality of the game, the pace, and the expectations that came with being a high draft pick. His rookie season averages of 8.2 points and 3.4 rebounds per game were modest, and the whispers of doubt grew louder. Critics questioned his durability, his defense, and whether he could be the cornerstone of a franchise.

However, beneath the surface of these early struggles, a transformation was underway. Dirk dedicated himself to his craft with amazing discipline. He spent countless hours refining his shot, expanding his range, and building his strength. The off-seasons were not times of rest but periods of intense improvement. His work ethic became the stuff of legend within the Mavericks organization, a showcase of his desire not just to belong but to excel.

The turn of the millennium marked the beginning of Dirk's rise to the top. By his third season (2000-2001), he was averaging 21.8 points per game, showcasing his unique skill set. He was not a traditional big man; he was an early leader of the "stretch four" gameplay, a power forward capable of scoring from anywhere on the court. His ability to shoot the three-pointer, drive to the basket, and utilize an unblockable fade-away shot made him a matchup nightmare.

The Dallas Mavericks, with Nowitzki as their leader, became a yearly contender in the Western Conference. Alongside Steve Nash and Michael Finley, he led the Mavericks to the playoffs year after year, but the ultimate prize remained out of reach. The early 2000s were full of near misses and playoff heartbreaks, each failure more painful than the last. The 2006 NBA Finals, in particular, was a crushing blow. The Mavericks, having secured a 2-0 series lead against the Miami Heat, slipped up, losing the next four games. The defeat was a bitter pill to swallow, with Dirk getting much of the blame.

The road to redemption was difficult. The Mavericks faced stiff competition from a Western Conference brimming with talent. Every season was a battle, every playoff series a war. Dirk's leadership, both on and off the court, was key to keeping the team focused, driven, and united in their singular goal: an NBA Championship. The 2010-2011 season was a showcase of Dirk's excellence and the result of years of hard work, both his and that of the Mavericks organization. The team, a blend of veterans and youth, was perfectly attuned to the challenges ahead.

They entered the playoffs as underdogs, a position that seemed to suit them just fine. The path to the Finals was a masterclass, with the Mavericks dispatching the Portland Trail Blazers, sweeping the defending champion Los Angeles Lakers, and overcoming the young Oklahoma City Thunder. Each series

was a showcase of Dirk's all-around skill set, his clutch performances in the fourth quarters becoming the stuff of legend.

Then came the rematch against the Miami Heat, now a jugger-
naut with the "Big Three" of LeBron James, Dwyane Wade,
and Chris Bosh. The narrative was irresistible: the seasoned
Mavericks, led by the battle-hardened Nowitzki, versus the
assembled might of Miami's superstars. It was a clash of
giants, of team basketball versus star power, of one man's
quest for redemption.

The Heat were favorites to win, having assembled a super
team that many thought would dominate the basketball world.
The series kicked off in Miami, where the Heat managed to
snatch the first game, showcasing their star power. However,
the Mavericks, showing incredible heart and teamwork, fought
back in Game 2 with Nowitzki leading a stunning comeback
to tie the series. The back-and-forth battle continued, with
each team grabbing victories, setting the stage for an unforgettable showdown. As the series progressed, the Mavericks
displayed extraordinary determination and skill, particularly
Nowitzki, who played through injury and illness, becoming a
true hero on the court.

The team's spirit was unmatched, with players like Jason Terry
and Tyson Chandler stepping up when it mattered most. With
the series tied 2-2, the Mavericks won Game 5, taking a
crucial lead. Heading back to Miami for Game 6, the Mave-

ricks were on the brink of making history, aiming to clinch their first-ever NBA Championship. It was a fairy tale in the making, and the stage was set for an epic finale that would captivate fans around the world.

The stage was set in Miami, Florida. The air was thick with anticipation as fans from all over the world tuned in to watch. The American Airlines Arena, home of the Heat, was packed to the rafters with excited spectators. Their cheers filled the air, creating a buzzing atmosphere that sent shivers down the spine. The Mavericks, led by their towering German superstar, stepped onto the court with one goal in mind: victory.

From the very beginning, the game was a rollercoaster of emotions. The Heat came out strong, showing why they were considered one of the best teams in the league. But the Mavericks were not intimidated. They had fought hard to get here, and they weren't about to give up now. Every time the Heat scored, the Mavericks responded. It was a battle of wills, a test of who wanted it more.

As the game progressed, Dirk Nowitzki began to shine. He was not just a player; he was a leader, a warrior on the court. Despite the immense pressure, he played with grace and skill that left everyone in awe.

His shots, a beautiful blend of power and precision, seemed to defy gravity, arcing through the air before swishing through the net. But this night was not just about Dirk's scoring. It was about his heart, his determination to carry his team to victory. With every play, he inspired his teammates, lifting their spirits and driving them forward. Whether it was a crucial rebound, a timely block, or a pass that set up a teammate for a basket, Dirk did it all.

The game was close, with the lead changing hands multiple times. As the clock ticked down, the tension became almost unbearable. The Mavericks clung to a slim lead, but with the Heat's talent, no lead was safe. The fans were on the edge of their seats, holding their breath with every shot, every pass.

Then, in the final minutes, Dirk took over. With the game hanging in the balance, he hit shot after shot, each one more improbable than the last. It was as if he had entered a zone where he was unstoppable, a place where legends are made. The Heat had no answer for him. With every basket, he brought the Mavericks closer to their dream.

Finally, as the buzzer sounded, the unimaginable had happened. The Dallas Mavericks had won, defeating the Miami Heat to become NBA Champions for the first time in franchise history. The arena fell silent, except for the cheers of the Mavericks and their fans. It was a moment of pure joy, a celebration of a dream realized after years of effort and determination.

Dirk Nowitzki, with tears in his eyes, was named the Finals MVP. It was a fitting honor for a player who had given his all, not just in this game, but throughout his career. His performance that night was a masterpiece, a testament to his skill, his heart, and his unwavering dedication to the game of basketball. As the Mavericks lifted the championship trophy high, confetti raining down upon them, the story of their victory became a beacon of hope and inspiration. It was a reminder that with hard work, perseverance, and a little bit of magic, anything is possible.

This was not just a victory for the Dallas Mavericks; it was a victory for every underdog who had ever dared to dream. Dirk Nowitzki, the boy from Germany, had led his team to the top. His journey, filled with ups and downs, had culminated in this perfect moment, a chapter in the story of the NBA that would be told for generations to come.

And so, as the Mavericks celebrated their triumph, the world celebrated with them. For on that warm June night in Miami, a legend was born, and a story of hope, courage, and determination unfolded—a story that would inspire young and old alike to reach for the stars and never give up on their dreams (Geoffreys, 2016).

CAREER HIGHLIGHTS

- Dirk began his professional career in the German basketball league (Bundesliga) before making the leap to the NBA.
- Nowitzki was selected 9th overall in the 1998 NBA Draft by the Milwaukee Bucks but was immediately traded to the Dallas Mavericks, where he spent his entire 21-season NBA career.
- Dirk led the Mavericks to their first and only NBA championship in 2011, earning Finals MVP honors for his dominant performance throughout the playoffs and the Finals against the Miami Heat's "Big Three."
- He was named the NBA Most Valuable Player (MVP) for the 2006-2007 season, becoming the first European player to win the award.
- Nowitzki finished his career with over 31,000 points, ranking him among the top scorers in NBA history. He is recognized for his scoring ability, particularly his signature fadeaway jump shot.
- Despite his height (7 feet tall), Nowitzki was an excellent three-point shooter, which helped revolutionize the power forward position by demonstrating the value of big men who could stretch the floor.
- Dirk had a significant impact on the international stage as well, leading the German national team to a

bronze medal in the 2002 FIBA World Championship and a silver medal in the 2005 EuroBasket, where he was also named the tournament's MVP.

The only advice I would give young guys is to keep your ears and eyes open. Never see yourself as a finished product.

DIRK NOWITZKI

CHAPTER 4
ALLEN IVERSON

OUR NEXT TALE BEGINS AND TAKES THE FORM OF A CLASSIC David versus Goliath story. On one side of the court, we had the monster that was Shaquille O'Neal, and his iconic Lakers, versus the incredibly skilled Allen Iverson. In the sprawling city of Los Angeles, under the bright lights of the Staples Center, an unforgettable tale of determination unfolded. It was a story that would echo through the halls of basketball history, inspiring countless fans and aspiring athletes around the world. This is the story of Allen Iverson and the Philadelphia 76ers during Game 1 of the 2001 NBA Finals, a tale that perfectly reflects the title of our book.

Allen Iverson, known as "The Answer" was not the tallest player on the court. Standing at just six feet tall, he was often overlooked because of his size. But what he lacked in height, he made up for with heart, skill, and an unbreakable spirit. The Los Angeles Lakers, with their towering duo of Shaquille O'Neal and Kobe Bryant, were the defending champions and had not lost a single game in the playoffs. They were giants in the land of basketball, seemingly unbeatable.

The game tipped off, and the Lakers quickly showed their strength. But the 76ers, led by Iverson, were not intimidated. He darted around the court like a lightning bolt, his quickness and agility a stark contrast to the power and size of the Lakers. As the game progressed, his performance became not just a display of skill, but a testament to perseverance.

Despite the Lakers' attempts to slow him down, Iverson kept scoring, his determination as evident as the sweat on his brow. With every basket, he seemed to say, "Size isn't everything. Heart matters more." His teammates, inspired by his leadership and grit, rallied around him. The 76ers' defense tightened, and the gap in the score began to close.

The game went back and forth, with the lead changing hands multiple times. As the final buzzer of regulation time sounded, the score was tied. The game would go into overtime. It was here, in these extra minutes, that Iverson's star shone the brightest.

In overtime, Iverson continued to defy the odds. With the game on the line, he made one of the most memorable plays in NBA history. After sinking a crucial shot, he stepped over Tyronn Lue of the Lakers, a moment captured in countless photographs and highlight reels. It was a bold statement, a symbol of Iverson's refusal to be overlooked or underestimated. The 76ers won the game 107-101, with Iverson scoring 48 points. It was a victory not just for Philadelphia but for underdogs everywhere. He had faced a team of giants and emerged victorious, his performance a brilliant display of courage and determination.

This game, especially his incredible performance, teaches us several important lessons. First, it shows us that challenges and obstacles can be overcome with hard work and perseverance. Iverson, despite being one of the smallest players on the court, used his skills and determination to lead his team to victory against all odds.

Unfortunately for Iverson and his 76ers, the Lakers, coached by the legendary Phil Jackson, rallied and swept the rest of the series. But it did nothing to take away from the incredible performance of Iverson. It further showed just how incredible it was to take on one of the best teams of all time and come out on top. For me, this is one of his most memorable performances, and this story made him an easy choice to join our list of inspirational stories, but this was just a moment in the incredible career of "The Answer".

Let's take a look at the rest of his incredible journey.

In the heart of Hampton, Virginia, a star was born. Allen Iverson, known for his incredible skill on the basketball court, began his journey in a world filled with challenges. His story is one of determination, resilience, and an undying belief in oneself, making it a beacon of inspiration for young dreamers everywhere. From a young age, he faced more hurdles than most. Growing up in a struggling household, Iverson quickly learned the value of hard work. His mother, Ann Iverson, was just 15 years old when she brought him into the world, instilling in him a fighter's spirit from the start. Despite the hardships, his love for sports, particularly football and basketball, shone brightly as a beacon of hope and a way out of adversity.

At Bethel High School, his athletic prowess became impossible to ignore. He led his school's football team to a state championship as a quarterback and did the same on the basketball court, showcasing a rare talent to excel at the highest levels in two demanding sports.

Iverson's undeniable talent on the basketball court led him to Georgetown University, where he played under the legendary coach John Thompson. Thompson became a mentor and father figure to him, providing the guidance and support he desperately needed. At Georgetown, his star continued to rise. He was named the Big East Rookie of the Year and set a school record for the scoring average by a freshman.

In his sophomore year, he led the Hoyas to the Elite Eight in the NCAA tournament and was named a First Team All-American. Iverson's collegiate career was marked by breathtaking plays, incredible scoring runs, and a passion for the game that was unmatched. As his collegiate journey at Georgetown came to a close, the next chapter of his life was about to be written on the grand stage of the NBA. Drafted first overall by the Philadelphia 76ers in the 1996 NBA Draft, Iverson stepped into the league with expectations as high as the skyscrapers in downtown Philadelphia. Yet, what awaited was a career so illustrious, so filled with heart, determination, and sheer talent, that it would forever change the game of basketball.

From the moment he set foot on the NBA hardwood, it was clear that the league had never seen a player quite like him. Standing at just six feet tall, he wasn't the biggest player on the court, but what he lacked in size, he more than made up for in heart and skill. His rookie season was nothing short of spectacular, as he averaged an incredible 23.5 points per game, earning him the NBA Rookie of the Year award. His crossover dribble, especially the one he famously used against Michael Jordan, became the stuff of legend, a move that would be replicated on playgrounds around the world for years to come.

The 2000-2001 season would prove to be the peak of his career. He led the league in scoring with an average of 31.1 points per game and carried the 76ers to the top of the Eastern Conference.

Iverson's performances were a blend of artistry and athleticism, as he dazzled fans with his scoring, his quickness, and his uncanny ability to make shots from seemingly impossible angles. His efforts were rewarded with the NBA's Most Valuable Player (MVP) award, a testament to his incredible impact on the game.

Following his unforgettable performance in the 2001 NBA Finals, he continued to solidify his legacy as one of the most dynamic and influential players in the history of basketball. Despite the Philadelphia 76ers' loss to the Los Angeles Lakers, Iverson emerged from the series not just as a scoring champion but as a symbol of resilience and determination in the face of adversity.

In the seasons that followed the Finals, Iverson remained a force to be reckoned with. His scoring prowess was unmatched, leading the NBA in points per game for two more seasons (2001-2002 and 2004-2005). His style of play, characterized by his quickness, agility, and fearless approach to driving towards the basket, continued to dazzle fans and frustrate opponents. Beyond his scoring, he was a relentless competitor, often playing through injuries and demonstrating a commitment to the game that was both admirable and inspiring. His career, however, was not without its challenges. The following years saw the 76ers struggling to build a championship-contending team around him.

In December 2006, after more than a decade with Philadelphia, his journey took a dramatic turn when he was traded to the Denver Nuggets. The move marked the end of an era for both Iverson and the 76ers but also the beginning of a new chapter in his storied career. In Denver, Iverson found a new home and an opportunity to reinvent himself. Paired with Carmelo Anthony, one of the league's rising stars, he helped lead the Nuggets to consecutive playoff appearances. His time in Denver showcased his ability to adapt and thrive, even as the landscape around him changed.

As his career progressed, his journey through the NBA took him to multiple teams, including the Detroit Pistons, the Memphis Grizzlies, and ultimately a brief return to the Philadelphia 76ers. These later years were marked by a mix of achievements and obstacles. While his talent on the court was undeniable, he faced challenges adapting to new roles and teams, illustrating the complexities of an aging superstar navigating the twilight of his career in the league.

Throughout his career, Iverson was more than just a basketball player; he was a cultural icon. His influence extended beyond the hardwood floors of NBA arenas into the realms of fashion, music, and popular culture. Iverson was at the forefront of a movement that embraced tattoos, cornrows, and a hip-hop-influenced style, challenging traditional norms and paving the way for future generations of athletes to express their individuality.

In 2013, Allen Iverson officially announced his retirement from professional basketball. The decision marked the end of an era, but also a moment to reflect on the incredible impact he had on the sport and society. His career statistics are impressive: 24,368 points, 5,624 assists, and 11 All-Star appearances. Yet, his legacy is defined by more than numbers. He was a pioneer, a fighter, and a source of inspiration for countless individuals who saw in him the embodiment of perseverance and the pursuit of one's dreams against all odds.

In 2016, Iverson was inducted into the Naismith Memorial Basketball Hall of Fame, a fitting tribute to his remarkable career and contributions to the game. His emotional speech touched on his struggles, his achievements, and the people who supported him throughout his journey. His induction was a testament to his greatness on the court and his impact off it, securing his place among the legends of basketball (Geoffreys, 2014).

CAREER HIGHLIGHTS

- Iverson had a standout collegiate career at Georgetown University, where he was named a First Team All-American and won the Big East Defensive Player of the Year award twice.
- Iverson was selected with the 1st overall pick in the

1996 NBA Draft by the Philadelphia 76ers, one of the most storied draft classes in NBA history.

- He won the NBA Rookie of the Year Award in 1997, immediately showcasing his scoring prowess and dynamic playmaking abilities.
- Iverson won four scoring titles throughout his career (1999, 2001, 2002, 2005), demonstrating his ability to score from anywhere on the court despite his size.
- Iverson was named the NBA MVP in 2001, leading the Philadelphia 76ers to the NBA Finals that same year.
- Iverson represented the United States at the 2004 Athens Olympics, winning a bronze medal.
- Iverson was inducted into the Naismith Memorial Basketball Hall of Fame in 2016, solidifying his legacy as one of the greatest guards to ever play the game.

I play every game like it's my last

ALLEN IVERSON

CHAPTER 5
LEBRON JAMES

As the Cleveland Cavaliers faced off against the Golden State Warriors in Game 7 of the NBA Finals, the air was thick with tension. The Cavaliers had done the unthinkable, clawing their way back from a 3-1 series deficit, something no team had achieved in the Finals. The stage was set for a showdown that would forever be remembered in basketball history.

Oracle Arena, the home of the Warriors, was a cauldron of anticipation, its fans split between belief and dread. The Warriors, having set the record for the most wins in a regular season, were on the brink of capping it with a championship, yet the Cavaliers, led by LeBron James, had momentum on their side. The game did not disappoint. It was a tightly contested affair, with both teams exchanging leads like heavyweight fighters trading blows. LeBron was everywhere—scoring, rebounding, and dishing out assists. His counterpart, Steph Curry, the league's reigning MVP, dazzled with his shooting prowess, keeping the Warriors in contention.

As the final quarter dwindled down, the score was knotted, and every possession became a battle. With less than two minutes to go, the Warriors initiated a fast break, Andre Iguodala driving to the basket, a clear path seemingly ahead for a layup to take the lead.

Then, in a moment that would define his legacy, LeBron, who had been on the opposite end of the court, sprinted back in a desperate bid to thwart the score. As Iguodala went up for the layup, LeBron soared, timing his jump with precision and power, his right hand smashing the ball against the backboard in a chase-down block that sent shockwaves through the arena and the millions watching around the globe. The block was more than just another defensive play; it was a statement, a showing of sheer will and determination.

LeBron's hustle back on defense represented the Cavaliers' resilience, their refusal to give in despite the odds stacked against them. As the ball was swatted away, the arena fell into a stunned silence, the Cavaliers' bench erupting in disbelief and joy. The game was still tied, but the momentum had shifted. The Cavaliers had the ball, and with it, a chance to take the lead.

The following moments were a blur of motion, the Cavaliers moving the ball with purpose, every player aware of the gravity of the moment. The shot clock ticked down, the ball found its way to Kyrie Irving, who, with Curry in his face, dribbled, stepped back, and released a three-pointer that seemed to hang in the air for an eternity.

This, my dear friends, is the story of how LeBron James not only became the best player of his generation but returned to his home state and brought back hope to Cleveland. But before we check back into our story, we need to understand the journey of LeBron to this moment.

LeBron's childhood in Akron, Ohio, was a testament to resilience and hope. Born on December 30, 1984, to Gloria James, who was just 16 at the time, his early life was marked by instability and struggle. Gloria, a single mother, worked tirelessly to provide for her son, moving from apartment to apartment in search of a better life. Despite the challenges, LeBron found peace and purpose on the basketball courts of Akron.

His incredible talent was evident from a young age, as he dominated youth leagues and attracted the attention of scouts across the nation. The hardships of his upbringing instilled in him a work ethic and determination that would become the hallmark of his career, driving him to reach the pinnacle of basketball greatness while never forgetting the community that shaped him.

His high school basketball career at St. Vincent-St. Mary High School in Akron, Ohio, was nothing short of legendary, quickly transforming him from a local prodigy into a national sensation. From his freshman year, LeBron's dominance on the court was unmistakable, leading his team to three state championships in four years and amassing a staggering array of personal accolades. His game was mature beyond his years, characterized by incredible athleticism, vision, and an innate understanding of basketball.

His performances were so compelling that some of his games had to be moved to the University of Akron's larger arena to accommodate the massive crowds that came to witness his talent. His senior year finished with him being named the Gatorade National Player of the Year for the second consecutive time, a rare feat that underscored his readiness for the professional leagues. His high school career was not just about the points he scored or the titles he won; it was a display of leadership, the ability to elevate those around him, and a clear signal that a generational talent was about to enter the NBA.

LeBron entered the NBA with expectations that few athletes in history have ever faced. Selected first overall in the 2003 NBA Draft by the Cleveland Cavaliers, he was immediately called the savior of the franchise, a beacon of hope for a city longing for a championship. His impact was instantaneous; he won the NBA Rookie of the Year Award, showcasing a blend of athleticism, intelligence, and leadership that was rare for a player straight out of high school.

In the years that followed, he rapidly ascended to the top of the NBA, his game evolving with each season. He transformed the Cavaliers into yearly contenders, leading them to the play-offs time after time and exciting fans with his incredible performances. In 2007, he carried Cleveland to its first NBA Finals appearance in franchise history. Though they were swept by the San Antonio Spurs, the feat was a testament to LeBron's singular talent and determination.

Despite his individual success, including two MVP awards in 2009 and 2010, a championship eluded him in Cleveland. The team's inability to secure a strong supporting cast for him contributed to mounting frustration. This period was characterized by breathtaking basketball, but also by the growing realization that LeBron might need to seek a new path to achieve his ultimate goal. The decision to leave Cleveland came in the summer of 2010, in a television special known as "The Decision."

LeBron announced he would be "taking his talents to South Beach" to join the Miami Heat, forming a super-team along-side Dwyane Wade and Chris Bosh. The move was controversial, sparking intense debate and criticism, yet it marked a new chapter in his career.

In Miami, LeBron's game reached new heights. Under the pressure of immense scrutiny, he matured both on and off the court. The Heat reached the NBA Finals in each of his four seasons with the team, winning back-to-back championships in 2012 and 2013. He was named Finals MVP both times, fulfilling the promise of his talent and silencing many of his critics. His time in Miami was a period of growth, overcoming challenges, and ultimately, triumph.

LeBron's return to Cleveland in the summer of 2014 was a historic event in the NBA, transcending sports to become a symbol of redemption and forgiveness. Announced through a heartfelt essay that emphasized his deep connection to Northeast Ohio, his decision to come back to the Cavaliers was motivated by more than basketball; it was about fulfilling a promise to bring a championship to his home region. This return immediately transformed the Cavaliers into title contenders and re-energized a fan base that had felt betrayed by his departure four years earlier. His impact was immediate, both on and off the court. He led by example, elevating the play of his teammates and taking the Cavaliers to four straight NBA Finals appearances from 2015 to 2018.

The 2016 NBA Finals will forever be remembered in basketball history, a series that epitomized drama, skill, and an undying will to win, largely scripted by LeBron and the Cleveland Cavaliers. Their opponent, the Golden State Warriors, had completed a record-setting 73-9 regular season, positioning themselves as formidable opponents. This series was not just a battle for the championship; it was a clash of legacies.

The Finals opened at Oracle Arena, where the Warriors' sharp-shooting prowess was on full display. Steph Curry and Klay Thompson, known as the "Splash Brothers," combined for a barrage of three-pointers that overwhelmed the Cavaliers. Despite LeBron's 23 points, 12 rebounds, and 9 assists, Cleveland fell 104-89. The Warriors' bench outscored the Cavaliers' reserves, highlighting the depth of Golden State's roster.

Game 2 saw the Warriors extend their dominance, winning 110-77. Draymond Green led the way with 28 points, including five three-pointers. The Cavaliers struggled offensively, their rhythm disrupted by Golden State's aggressive defense. LeBron's efforts were again notable but insufficient against the Warriors' collective performance. The series appeared to be slipping away from Cleveland, with many questioning their ability to respond. Back in Cleveland for Game 3, the Cavaliers showcased their resilience. LeBron and Kyrie Irving combined for 62 points, propelling Cleveland to a 120-90 victory. The Cavaliers' defense intensified, stifling the

Warriors' offense and cutting the series deficit to 2-1. This game served as a reminder of Cleveland's capabilities, reigniting hope among their fans.

Game 4 presented an opportunity for the Cavaliers to level the series, but the Warriors had other plans. Curry found his rhythm, scoring 38 points in a 108-97 victory for Golden State. The Warriors' precision from beyond the arc was the difference, as they set a Finals record with 17 three-pointers. The Cavaliers faced a daunting 3-1 series deficit, a situation from which no team had ever recovered in the NBA Finals.

Facing elimination, LeBron and Kyrie Irving put forth historic performances in Game 5, each scoring 41 points in a 112-97 win. Their dual heroics were unprecedented in Finals history and kept Cleveland's championship hopes alive. The Cavaliers' aggressive play and improved defense were key factors, as they benefited from Draymond Green's suspension for too many technical fouls.

Back in Cleveland for Game 6, LeBron James delivered another 41-point masterpiece, complemented by Irving's 23 points, to lead the Cavaliers to a 115-101 victory. The Cavaliers' energy and determination forced a series-deciding Game 7. LeBron's back-to-back 41-point games were a testament to his greatness and set the stage for a historic finale. Finally, we return to where we began our story. LeBron James had made one of the greatest blocks in NBA history, and Kyrie had just released a three-point effort in the face of Steph Curry.

As the ball arced towards the basket, Oracle Arena held its breath, the arena a mix of nerves and excitement. This shot wasn't just a potential game-winner; it was a moment that could define careers and legacies. Kyrie Irving, with ice in his veins, watched alongside everyone else as the ball traced its path towards destiny. Stephen Curry, one of the best shooters the game has ever seen, could only watch, having contested the shot as best he could without fouling.

The silence was deafening, a stark contrast to the noise that had filled the arena moments before. Time seemed to slow as the ball reached the top of its arc, the fate of the championship hanging in the balance. On the Cavaliers' bench, players and coaches linked arms, their expressions a mix of hope and worry. In Cleveland and across the nation, fans of the Cavaliers held their breath, their hopes pinned on the flight of a basketball.

Then, in a moment that seemed to freeze time, the ball swished through the net. The silence in Oracle Arena was shattered by the roar of the Cavaliers' bench and the stunned gasps of the Warriors' fans. Kyrie Irving's three-pointer had found its mark, giving the Cavaliers a crucial lead with less than a minute left on the clock.

The Warriors, now trailing, scrambled to respond. The Cavaliers' defense, strengthened by LeBron's amazing block and Irving's incredible shot, tightened. Every pass, every movement was contested with a ferocity that had defined the series.

The Warriors, a team known for their control and ability to score under pressure, found themselves up against a wall that refused to budge.

As the final seconds ticked away, the Cavaliers managed to maintain their lead. When the buzzer finally sounded, the realization of what had been achieved began to sink in. The Cleveland Cavaliers had completed the greatest comeback in NBA Finals history, overturning a 3-1 deficit against a team that had been considered one of the greatest ever assembled.

The Cavaliers' bench erupted, players and staff storming the court in a deluge of emotion. LeBron, tears streaming down his face, fell to his knees, the weight of his promise to bring a championship to Cleveland fulfilled. The Warriors, gracious in defeat, could only watch as the Cavaliers celebrated, their dream of back-to-back championships dashed in the most dramatic of fashions.

This victory was more than just a championship win; it was proof that LeBron James made the right decision to return to Cleveland, a testament to the resilience of the team, and a story of redemption and determination that would be told for generations to come. The 2016 NBA Finals had indeed been etched into the annals of basketball history, not just for the quality of the games, but for the incredible journey of the Cleveland Cavaliers, who had dared to believe in the impossible (The Editors of Encyclopaedia Britannica).

CAREER HIGHLIGHTS

- LeBron was a prodigy at St. Vincent-St. Mary High School, where he was heavily spotlighted by the national media.
- LeBron was selected with the 1st overall pick in the 2003 NBA Draft by the Cleveland Cavaliers.
- He won the NBA Rookie of the Year Award in 2004, immediately establishing himself as one of the league's premier talents.
- LeBron has won multiple NBA championships, showcasing his leadership and ability to excel on the biggest stage. He won two titles with the Miami Heat (2012, 2013), one with the Cleveland Cavaliers (2016), and one with the Los Angeles Lakers (2020).
- James has been named NBA Finals MVP multiple times, underlining his pivotal role in his teams' championship runs.
- LeBron has won the NBA Most Valuable Player (MVP) Award four times (2009, 2010, 2012, 2013), demonstrating his all-around excellence and impact on the game.
- LeBron has amassed over 40,000 points, making him the top scorer in NBA history. He's also known for his playmaking ability, consistently ranking high in assists.

- LeBron has represented the United States in the Olympics, winning gold medals in 2008 (Beijing) and 2012 (London), and a bronze in 2004 (Athens).
- LeBron's career is characterized not just by his statistical achievements but also by his leadership, versatility, and longevity in the league. He has influenced the game significantly, from how teams are built to how players approach their careers and ventures beyond basketball.

 CLEVELAND!! This is for you.

LEBRON JAMES

CHAPTER 6
JEREMY LIN

IN THE HEART OF THE 2011-2012 NBA SEASON, AN underdog story began to unfold, one that would captivate the world and etch its main character, Jeremy Lin, into sports history forever. This story is dedicated to "Linsanity" a phenomenon that transcended basketball, showcasing an incredible rise from unknown to superstar.

Before Linsanity could take the world by storm, Jeremy Lin's journey was filled with rejection, doubt, and perseverance. Lin, an undrafted guard out of Harvard, found little interest from NBA teams, facing low expectations due to his Asian American heritage. He bounced around the league, being cut by the Golden State Warriors and the Houston Rockets, before landing a non-guaranteed contract with the New York Knicks. His early days with the Knicks were far from glamorous. He was on the verge of being cut again and was sleeping on his brother's couch, uncertain of his NBA future.

On February 4, 2012, the Knicks faced the New Jersey Nets in what seemed like another routine game in a struggling season. However, fate had a different script in mind. With the Knicks' stars out and the team struggling, coach Mike D'Antoni looked down his bench and decided to give Lin a chance.

He seized the opportunity with both hands. He scored 25 points, handed out 7 assists, and grabbed 5 rebounds, leading the Knicks to a much-needed victory. This performance was not just a personal triumph; it was a beacon of hope for the team. Lin's energy, fearlessness, and leadership on the court were infectious. His ability to penetrate defenses, his court vision, and his clutch scoring inspired the Knicks, setting the stage for what was to come.

The Nets game proved to be just the beginning. Lin's confidence soared, and D'Antoni kept him in the starting lineup.

What followed was a stretch of games that can only be described as magical. He continued to defy expectations, leading the Knicks on a seven-game winning streak.

During this run, his performances were nothing short of spectacular. He scored 28 points against the Utah Jazz, 23 points against the Washington Wizards, and an unforgettable 38 points against the Los Angeles Lakers. Lin's knack for hitting big shots, and his humble personality won over fans and players alike. To fully appreciate the phenomenon that was Linsanity, we need to take a closer look at this 38-point game against the Lakers because it's not every day that an undrafted guard manages to outduel the great Kobe Bryant on the national stage.

On a crisp February night in 2012, Madison Square Garden was buzzing with anticipation. The New York Knicks were set to face the Los Angeles Lakers, a formidable opponent led by Kobe. This was not just another game on the calendar; it was the stage for what would become the apex of Linsanity, a chapter where Jeremy Lin's fairy tale journey would collide with basketball royalty. As fans filled the stands, the air was thick with excitement and curiosity. Jeremy Lin, the undrafted Harvard graduate who had captured the hearts of fans worldwide, was about to face his toughest challenge yet.

The Lakers, with their championship pedigree, represented a test for his blossoming legend. Could the Cinderella story continue against one of the NBA's most storied franchises?

Despite the magnitude of the game and the spotlight on him, Lin approached the contest with his characteristic humility and unshakeable confidence. In the days leading up to the game, Kobe Bryant had famously said he had no idea who Lin was or what he had been accomplishing. This perceived insult only added fuel to Lin's fire, though he remained outwardly calm and focused on the task at hand.

From the opening tip, it was clear that this was his night. He dazzled the crowd with his quickness, court vision, and scoring ability. Lin was everywhere, slicing through the Lakers' defense, hitting jump shots, and finding teammates for easy baskets. Each basket he scored sent waves of excitement through the Garden, as fans began to believe that they were witnessing something truly special.

Lin's performance was not just about scoring; it was about leadership. With each play, he inspired his teammates, elevating their play and forging a unity that had been missing from the Knicks' season. His energy was infectious, and as the game progressed, it became clear that the Knicks were not just competing with the Lakers—they were dominating them. The game was also marked by the intriguing matchup between him and Kobe.

While Bryant was already an established legend of the game, Lin was the upstart making headlines around the world. Their interactions on the court were a fascinating subplot, with Lin not backing down and Bryant, in turn, recognizing the challenge and stepping up his game.

Despite Bryant's efforts and his game-high 34 points, the night belonged to Lin. He outplayed the Lakers' star in the context that mattered most—leading his team to victory. He finished the game with 38 points, 7 assists, and 4 rebounds, outscoring Bryant and cementing his place in the hearts of Knicks fans and basketball enthusiasts worldwide.

The Knicks' 92-85 victory over the Lakers was more than just a win in the regular season; it was a statement. Jeremy Lin had not only stood up to one of the NBA's best teams but had also shone brightest on one of the biggest stages. Post-game, Kobe Bryant expressed his admiration for Lin's performance, acknowledging his talent and the incredible journey he was on. But Linsanity was far from over. Jeremy Lin, the unheralded hero of the New York Knicks, continued his stunning performances with a game-winner against the Toronto Raptors.

It was a chilly evening in Toronto, the kind of night that seemed designed for indoor sports. Inside the echoing Raptors' home court, fans buzzed with excitement. The New York Knicks, led by the surprisingly sensational Lin, were locked in a tight game against the Raptors.

Jeremy Lin, whose journey to this moment had been anything but normal, found himself in a position to prove that miracles could happen on a basketball court. Undrafted, overlooked, and nearly cut from the team, Lin's rise was the stuff of fairy tales. The game against the Raptors was tied, with the clock winding down to its final seconds. The air was thick with tension, every heartbeat in the arena seemingly in sync, waiting for the final play.

The Knicks had the ball, and as they called a timeout to set up the play, Lin's coach didn't hesitate. He knew who he wanted to have the ball in this important moment. Jeremy Lin was their man. Despite his inexperience, Lin had shown a knack for rising to the occasion.

As the players returned to the court, Lin received the inbound pass. The crowd rose to their feet, a mixture of Raptors fans hoping for a defensive stop and Knicks fans praying for another miracle. Lin dribbled near half court, the seconds ticking away. His teammates spread out, giving him space to operate. The Raptors' best defender eyed him warily, ready to pounce at any sign of weakness.

But Lin wasn't thinking about the defender in front of him or the thousands of eyes fixed on his every move. He was in his zone, a place of pure focus where the noise and pressure faded into the background. With the clock down to its final five seconds, Lin began his move.

He feinted left, then stepped back beyond the three-point line. The defender, caught off guard, scrambled to close the gap, but it was too late. Lin gathered himself and launched the ball into the air with a flick of his wrist, a motion he had practiced thousands of times in empty gyms and crowded arenas alike. Time seemed to stand still as the ball arced gracefully towards the basket. The crowd held its breath, the outcome of the game hanging in the balance. And then, as if guided by some unseen hand, the ball swished through the net. The buzzer sounded, signaling the end of the game. The Knicks had won, thanks to Jeremy Lin's incredible buzzer-beater.

The arena erupted into chaos. Knicks fans screamed in cele-bration, while Raptors supporters stood in stunned silence. Lin's teammates rushed the court, lifting him into the air, their faces alight with joy and disbelief. It was a moment of pure ecstasy, a reminder of why sports can captivate and inspire like nothing else. Lin's time with the Knicks would eventually come to an end, but his impact on the game and on millions of fans around the world would not be forgotten. Linsanity was more than just a string of great basketball games; it was a story of determination, perseverance, and the power of belief.

Lin's journey from sleeping on his brother's couch to becoming an NBA sensation is a powerful reminder that no dream is too big, and no obstacle is insurmountable. He showed that with hard work, faith, and a never-give-up atti-tude, anything is possible.

For every young person reading this chapter, let Jeremy Lin's story be a beacon of hope and inspiration. Whether your dreams lie in sports, academics, arts, or any other field, remember that success is not just about talent; it's about perseverance, hard work, and the courage to chase your dreams, even when the odds seem stacked against you.

Jeremy Lin's legacy goes beyond basketball. It's a testament to the human spirit's resilience and the incredible things we can achieve when we believe in ourselves. So, as you face challenges and pursue your dreams, remember the story of Linsanity—a tale of an underdog who dared to dream big and, through sheer determination and faith, turned those dreams into reality (Chin, 2022).

CAREER HIGHLIGHTS

- Lin played college basketball for Harvard University, where he was a standout player but did not get drafted in the 2010 NBA Draft.
- Lin signed with his hometown Golden State Warriors in 2010 as an undrafted free agent, beginning his professional career with limited playing time and being assigned to the D-League multiple times.
- Lin's rise to fame occurred in February 2012 with the New York Knicks, where, due to injuries to key players, he was given significant playing time and sparked a winning streak, scoring 20 or more points in several consecutive games. This period, known as

"Linsanity," captured the attention of basketball fans worldwide and highlighted Lin's scoring ability, playmaking skills, and clutch performances.

- After his breakout season, Lin signed with the Houston Rockets and later played for several other teams, including the Los Angeles Lakers, Charlotte Hornets, Brooklyn Nets, Atlanta Hawks, and Toronto Raptors, contributing as a solid role player and mentor to younger teammates.
- Lin won an NBA Championship with the Toronto Raptors in 2019, becoming the first Asian American to win an NBA title.
- After his time in the NBA, Lin played in the Chinese Basketball Association (CBA) for the Beijing Ducks, showcasing his talent and leadership on an international stage.

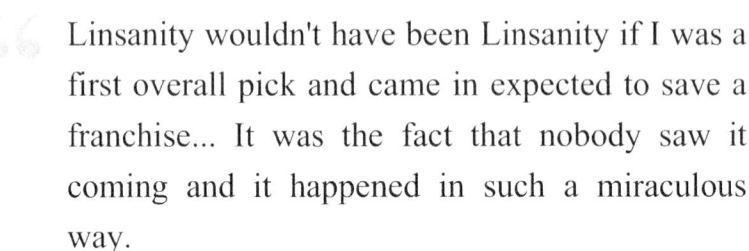

Linsanity wouldn't have been Linsanity if I was a first overall pick and came in expected to save a franchise... It was the fact that nobody saw it coming and it happened in such a miraculous way.

JEREMY LIN

CHAPTER 7
MICHAEL JORDAN

MY FRIENDS, THIS IS THE TALE OF THE GREATEST BASKETBALL player to ever lace up a pair of shoes. A man who was not born great, but through his incredible work ethic, unbreakable mindset, and belief in himself transformed into the ultimate winner and one of the most iconic figures in sports history. This is the story of Michael Jordan.

Born on February 17, 1963, in Brooklyn, New York, Michael Jeffrey Jordan was the fourth of five children of James and Deloris Jordan. The Jordan family moved to Wilmington, North Carolina, when Michael was still a toddler. This shift from the bustling streets of Brooklyn to the more serene environment of Wilmington would play a significant role in shaping his early experiences and, eventually, his path to basketball greatness.

Jordan's affinity for sports was evident from an early age, but it was the competitive environment of his household that truly honed his desire to excel. His father, James Jordan, was instrumental in nurturing Michael's competitiveness, often engaging him in various sports, including basketball and baseball. His mother, Deloris, instilled in him the value of hard work and education, lessons that Michael would carry throughout his life.

However, his journey to basketball stardom was not without its challenges. At Laney High School in Wilmington, as a teenager, Jordan was famously cut from the varsity basketball team during his sophomore year because he was deemed too short at 5'11". This setback became an important moment in his life, fueling his determination to prove his doubters wrong. He spent the summer before his junior year training and grew four inches taller, which, combined with his newfound skills and determination, earned him a spot on the varsity squad the following season.

His junior and senior years at Laney High School were marked by remarkable performances that caught the attention of college scouts across the nation. He averaged over 25 points per game in both seasons, showcasing not just his scoring ability but also his versatility on the court. His senior season was particularly outstanding, as he was selected to the McDonald's All-American Team, putting him among the top high school basketball players in the country.

Jordan's college career at the University of North Carolina at Chapel Hill under legendary coach Dean Smith was both formative and spectacular. As a freshman, he made an immediate impact on the team, which was already loaded with talent, including James Worthy and Sam Perkins. It was during the 1982 NCAA Championship game against Georgetown that his knack for clutch performances began to emerge. With 17 seconds left on the clock and North Carolina trailing by one, he hit the game-winning jump shot, securing the national championship for the Tar Heels and announcing his arrival on the big stage.

During his three seasons at UNC, Jordan's game flourished under Smith's guidance. He was named the NCAA College Player of the Year in both his sophomore and junior years and won the Naismith and the Wooden College Player of the Year awards in 1984. Off the court, his commitment to his studies, a value instilled in him by his parents, remained steadfast.

Jordan's decision to leave UNC after his junior year and enter the 1984 NBA Draft marked the end of his college career but the beginning of an incredible professional journey. The Chicago Bulls selected him with the third overall pick, a decision that would change the fortune of the franchise and the landscape of the NBA forever.

Michael's transition from a collegiate star to an NBA rookie was met with great anticipation and excitement. When he was drafted by the Chicago Bulls, the team was in need of a turnaround. The Bulls had not experienced significant success in years, and Jordan was viewed as the beacon of hope for a franchise full of mediocrity. Little did anyone know, he would not only transform the Bulls but also leave an unforgettable mark on the NBA and the sport of basketball worldwide.

Jordan's impact on the league was immediate. In his rookie season, he averaged an impressive 28.2 points per game, earning him the NBA Rookie of the Year award and a spot on the All-Star team. His athletic prowess, scoring ability, and competitive spirit quickly made him a fan favorite, not just in Chicago but across the globe. His style of play, characterized by his gravity-defying dunks, unmatched defensive skills, and the ability to score from virtually anywhere on the court, electrified audiences and rejuvenated the Bulls' fan base.

However, his early years in the NBA were not just about personal accolades. He was determined to lead the Bulls to team success.

Despite his individual brilliance, the Bulls struggled to make deep playoff runs in Jordan's first few seasons. The Eastern Conference was dominated by powerhouse teams like the Boston Celtics and the Detroit Pistons, and the Bulls had to contend with these formidable foes.

The battles with the Detroit Pistons, in particular, became legendary. The Pistons, known as the "Bad Boys" for their physical style of play, were a significant hurdle for Jordan and the Bulls. From 1988 to 1990, the Bulls faced the Pistons in the playoffs three consecutive years, each meeting more intense and physical than the last. The Pistons employed a defensive strategy known as the "Jordan Rules," which was designed to contain Michael by using physical play to wear him down and force him into tough shots or pass the ball.

These encounters with the Pistons were brutal and often left Jordan battered and bruised. However, they were instrumental in shaping his resolve and understanding of what it took to win at the highest level. The repeated playoff failures against the Pistons taught him the importance of teamwork and defense, lessons that he took to heart and applied not just to his game but to his leadership of the Bulls.

The turning point came in the 1990-1991 season. Under the guidance of Phil Jackson, who became the head coach in 1989, and with the emergence of Scottie Pippen as a star in his own right, the Bulls evolved into a more balanced and formidable team.

Jordan's willingness to trust his teammates and embrace Jackson's triangle offense played a crucial role in transforming the Bulls into a championship-caliber team.

The 1991 Eastern Conference Finals against the Pistons was the ultimate test of his growth as a player and leader. The Bulls swept the Pistons in four games, a symbolic passing of the torch in the Eastern Conference. The series was not just a victory over a rival; it was a statement by Jordan and the Bulls that they had arrived. His battles with the Pistons had finally culminated in triumph, setting the stage for the Bulls' dynasty in the 1990s.

The 1990-1991 season was a turning point for the Bulls. With the defeat of their arch-nemesis, the Detroit Pistons, in the Eastern Conference Finals, the Bulls advanced to the NBA Finals for the first time in Michael's career. Their opponents, the Los Angeles Lakers, led by Magic Johnson, were experienced champions. However, the Bulls, under Phil Jackson's leadership, were ready. Jordan's outstanding performance, including a spectacular switch-hand layup in Game 2, highlighted his versatility and skill. The Bulls won the series 4-1, and Jordan, who averaged 31.2 points, 6.6 rebounds, 11.4 assists, and 2.8 steals per game, was named Finals MVP. This victory was not just a personal triumph for him but a collective achievement for the Bulls, signaling the rise of a new power in the NBA.

Entering the 1991-1992 season as reigning champions, the Bulls were the team to beat. They embraced this challenge with relentless determination. The regular season saw him leading the league in scoring for the sixth straight year, and the Bulls finishing with a 67-15 record, the best in the league. The playoffs tested the Bulls' resilience, particularly in the fiercely contested NBA Finals against the Portland Trail Blazers and Clyde Drexler, one of the few players at the time who could be compared to Michael in talent and ability.

In Game 1, Jordan silenced any debate about his supremacy by setting a Finals record with six three-pointers in the first half, famously shrugging as if to say he couldn't believe his own performance. The Bulls clinched their second consecutive championship in six games, with Jordan again named Finals MVP.

Achieving back-to-back championships was a formidable feat, but securing a three-peat would elevate the Bulls to legendary status. The 1992-1993 season was marked by the Bulls' unwavering focus and the growing legacy of Michael Jordan. Despite facing strong challenges throughout the regular season and the playoffs, the Bulls' championship experience and Jordan's leadership shone through. The Phoenix Suns, led by Charles Barkley, the MVP of the regular season, were their opponents in the NBA Finals. The series was a showcase of Jordan's scoring prowess; he averaged a Finals-record 41.0 points per game over the six-game series.

The Bulls clinched their third consecutive championship on a John Paxson three-pointer in Game 6, with Michael securing his third consecutive Finals MVP award.

This first three-peat was a testament to Michael Jordan's greatness and the collective strength of the Chicago Bulls. His leadership, scoring ability, and defensive prowess were unparalleled, but the contributions of Scottie Pippen, Horace Grant, John Paxson, and others were equally vital. Phil Jackson's coaching philosophy and the triangle offense were instrumental in harnessing the talent of the team to achieve their common goal. The first three-peat not only solidified the Bulls' dynasty but also cemented Michael Jordan's legacy.

The peak of Jordan's basketball career was abruptly halted by personal tragedy in the summer of 1993. On July 23, the Jordan family received the heartbreaking news that his father had passed away. This devastating event shook Jordan to his core, as he shared an exceptionally close bond with his father, who had been a guiding light throughout his life and career. James Jordan's death profoundly impacted Michael, leading him to reevaluate his life and career priorities.

In a move that shocked the world, Michael announced his retirement from basketball on October 6, 1993. At the peak of his game and following a historic three-peat championship run with the Chicago Bulls, his decision to step away from the NBA was incomprehensible to many.

However, he cited the loss of his desire to play basketball and the impact of his father's death as primary reasons for his retirement. He expressed the need to find joy and fulfillment in other aspects of his life, away from the basketball court.

His father had once expressed a desire for him to play baseball, a sport they both loved and shared. Honoring this wish and seeking a new challenge, Jordan pursued a career in professional baseball, a decision that further astonished fans and media alike. In February 1994, he signed a minor league baseball contract with the Chicago White Sox, an MLB team also owned by Jerry Reinsdorf, who owned the Bulls. He was assigned to the Birmingham Barons, the White Sox's Double-A affiliate, for the 1994 season.

Transitioning from basketball to baseball was a humbling journey for Jordan. Despite his athletic prowess, baseball presented a different set of challenges. His year with the Barons was marked by highs and lows; he struggled at times but also showed improvement and a commendable work ethic. He finished the season with a .202 batting average, three home runs, 51 RBIs, and 30 stolen bases. Beyond the statistics, Jordan's foray into baseball was a personal quest, a way to heal and honor his father's memory while exploring his own limits and passions outside basketball.

His time in baseball, while brief, exemplified his willingness to take risks and step outside his comfort zone.

It was a period of personal growth, reflection, and exploration that underscored the complexities of his character beyond his identity as a basketball icon. Jordan's venture into baseball, motivated by the loss of his father and a desire for a new beginning, remains a unique and poignant chapter in his remarkable life story.

Jordan's time in baseball was an important chapter in his storied career, a detour that reflected his personal struggles and a tribute to his late father. However, the basketball world's gravitational pull proved irresistible, leading to one of the most celebrated comebacks in sports history. In March 1995, Jordan announced his return to the NBA with two simple yet powerful words: "I'm back." This declaration sent waves of excitement throughout the sports community and reignited the competitive spirit of the Chicago Bulls.

His return to basketball during the latter part of the 1994-1995 NBA season was a momentous event. Although he showed signs of rust from his baseball sabbatical, his talent, drive, and leadership were undiminished. The Bulls, who had been competitive but not dominant in his absence, were instantly transformed back into championship contenders. However, the 1995 playoffs ended in disappointment for Jordan and the Bulls, as they fell to the Orlando Magic in the Eastern Conference Semifinals. This defeat served as a catalyst for Jordan, who dedicated himself to a full off-season of basketball training for the first time in two years.

The 1995-1996 season marked the beginning of the Bulls' second three-peat, a period of dominance that would etch the team's legacy into NBA lore. Jordan returned with a vengeance, leading the Bulls to an NBA-record 72 wins and a mere 10 losses during the regular season. His phenomenal performance earned him the MVP award for both the regular season and the NBA Finals. The Bulls capped off this historic year by defeating the Seattle SuperSonics in the Finals, securing Jordan's fourth championship and reaffirming his status as the game's premier player.

The following two seasons saw the Bulls continue their dominance. In the 1996-1997 season, the Bulls faced a formidable opponent in the Utah Jazz, led by Karl Malone and John Stockton, in the NBA Finals. The series was competitive and intense, featuring memorable moments such as Jordan's "flu game" in Game 5, where he played through illness to lead the Bulls to a crucial victory. The Bulls ultimately clinched their fifth championship in six years.

The 1997-1998 season, known as "The Last Dance," was the final chapter in the Bulls' dynasty. Amidst speculation about the team's future and tensions with the front office, Jordan and the Bulls remained focused on their ultimate goal. The Bulls once again faced the Jazz in the NBA Finals, in a repeat of the previous year's matchup. The series culminated in one of his most iconic moments: his game-winning shot over Bryon

Russell in Game 6, securing the Bulls' sixth championship in eight years and completing their second three-peat.

Jordan's second retirement from the Bulls in January 1999 marked the end of an era. His second stint in the NBA not only added to his collection of championships, MVP awards, and memorable moments but also solidified his legacy as one of the greatest competitors and basketball players of all time. The second three-peat was a testament to his unmatched skill, leadership, and determination, qualities that transcended the sport and inspired athletes and fans around the world. Michael Jordan's return to basketball and the subsequent second three-peat with the Chicago Bulls is a story of resilience, redemption, and the relentless pursuit of greatness (Piccotti, 2024).

CAREER HIGHLIGHTS

- Jordan played three seasons of college basketball at the University of North Carolina at Chapel Hill. He led the Tar Heels to the 1982 NCAA Championship, hitting the game-winning shot.
- Jordan was selected with the 3rd overall pick in the 1984 NBA Draft by the Chicago Bulls.
- He won the NBA Rookie of the Year Award in 1985 after an impressive debut season.
- Jordan led the Chicago Bulls to six NBA championships (1991-1993, 1996-1998), earning

Finals MVP in each appearance, a testament to his dominance and leadership.

- He was named the NBA Most Valuable Player (MVP) five times (1988, 1991, 1992, 1996, 1998), showcasing his all-around excellence and impact on the game.

- Jordan won a record 10 NBA scoring titles, highlighting his unparalleled offensive prowess.

- In 1988, Jordan was named the NBA Defensive Player of the Year, demonstrating his exceptional defensive abilities.

- Jordan won two Olympic gold medals with Team USA: first in 1984 in Los Angeles as a college player and then as part of the "Dream Team" in 1992 in Barcelona.

- Jordan was inducted into the Naismith Memorial Basketball Hall of Fame twice: once in 2009 for his individual career and again in 2010 as part of the "Dream Team."

- After retiring, Jordan became the majority owner of the Charlotte Hornets, contributing to the NBA from an executive standpoint.

- Jordan's competitiveness, style of play, and will to win have left a lasting legacy on the sport, making him an icon not only in basketball but in global sports culture.

Never say never, because limits, like fears, are often just an illusion.

MICHAEL JORDAN

CHAPTER 8
GIANNIS ANTETOKOUNMPO

In the heart of Athens, Greece, within the bustling neighborhood of Sepolia, a young boy named Giannis embarked on a journey that would transform him from a street vendor into an international basketball sensation. This is the story of Giannis Antetokounmpo, a tale woven with dreams, determination, and the undying spirit of a family bound by love and ambition.

GIANNIS ANTETOKOUNMPO
"THE GREEK FREAK"

Born on December 6, 1994, to Nigerian immigrants Charles and Veronica, the Antetokounmpo family's life was far from easy, with financial stability just a fleeting dream. Charles and Veronica struggled to find consistent work, a challenge compounded by their status as immigrants. The family's financial woes meant that Giannis and his brothers often took to the streets, selling watches, bags, and sunglasses to support their household. Despite the hardships, his childhood was rich in love and laughter. His parents instilled in him and his siblings the values of hard work, respect, and the importance of family. These lessons became the foundation upon which he built his future.

Basketball was not an immediate calling for Giannis. The sport was a distant reality, one that existed beyond the immediate needs of survival and supporting his family. However, fate intervened when he was introduced to basketball at the age of 12. The game offered a glimmer of hope, a potential escape from the hardships of daily life.

His introduction to basketball was not marked by immediate success. He possessed raw talent but lacked the formal training and resources that many of his peers had. His family could not afford basketball shoes or the fees for organized leagues. Yet, his passion for the game was undeniable. He spent countless hours practicing in local gyms and on outdoor courts, often playing in shoes that were too small or worn out.

The turning point in Giannis's life came when he joined Filathlitikos, a local youth team. It was here that his raw talent began to shine through. He was a quick learner, and his natural athleticism allowed him to excel rapidly. Despite the challenges, including language barriers and financial constraints, his dedication to the game did not waver. As Giannis grew older, so did his ambitions. He dreamed of playing professional basketball, a dream that seemed as distant as the stars. However, he was not alone in his journey. His family, particularly his older brother Thanasis, shared his dream. Together, they faced the challenges head-on, supporting each other through every challenge.

His dedication began to pay off. By his mid-teens, he had made a name for himself in the local basketball circles. Scouts and coaches began to take notice of the lanky teenager with an incredible work ethic and a relentless drive to improve. However, his journey was not without its setbacks. His undocumented status in Greece posed a significant barrier to advancing his career. Despite being born in Greece, Giannis and his brothers were not automatically granted citizenship due to their parents' immigration status.

The family's perseverance finally bore fruit when, at the age of 18, he received Greek citizenship. This fantastic occasion opened new doors for Giannis, allowing him to participate in tournaments and showcases beyond the borders of Greece.

His final year in high school was a turning point. His performance on the court was nothing short of spectacular. He dominated the competition, showcasing a unique blend of athleticism, skill, and basketball IQ. His ability to play multiple positions, coupled with his defensive prowess and offensive versatility, made him a standout player. The buzz around Giannis grew louder with each game. His story of overcoming adversity to chase his dream resonated with many. It wasn't long before he caught the attention of NBA scouts, intrigued by the young prospect from Greece with a heart-warming story and an amazing skill set.

In 2013, his dream became a reality when he declared for the NBA Draft. It was a bold move, one that carried the weight of his family's hopes and his own dreams. On draft night, Giannis, accompanied by his family, waited nervously. When the Milwaukee Bucks selected him with the 15th overall pick, it was a moment of pure joy and disbelief. His rookie season with the Milwaukee Bucks was a period of adaptation and growth. He quickly became known for his work ethic, humility, and eagerness to learn. On the court, he showed flashes of brilliance, his unique combination of length, athleticism, and versatility hinting at the superstar he could become.

The challenges, however, were plentiful. Adjusting to the pace and physicality of the NBA, learning a new culture, and dealing with the expectations of being a first-round pick were daunting tasks.

Yet, he approached each obstacle with determination and grace. His rookie season stats were modest, but his impact on the team and the promise he showed were significant. Giannis's dedication to improving his game was evident from the start. He spent countless hours in the gym, working on his shooting, ball-handling, and understanding of the game. His second season saw marked improvement, as he began to take on a more significant role within the team. His ability to impact the game in multiple ways—scoring, rebounding, defending—started to shine through.

It was during these early years that Giannis earned the nickname "The Greek Freak," a nod to his extraordinary physical attributes and his ability to do things on the court that few others could. Yet, despite his growing fame, he remained grounded, always remembering the struggles of his past and the reasons he played the game. With each passing season, his game continued to evolve. His hard work and dedication were paying off, as he transformed from a promising young talent into one of the league's most dominant players. This rise was incredible, his performances captivating fans and analysts alike. He was not just a scorer; he was a playmaker, a defender, and a leader on and off the court.

The 2016-2017 season marked a turning point in The Greek Freak's career. He was named to his first All-Star game, a recognition of his status as one of the best talents in the league.

His stats across the board were impressive, earning him the Most Improved Player award. He had not only lived up to the potential seen in him on draft night but had surpassed expectations, setting new standards for himself and for those who followed in his footsteps. His ascent to the pinnacle of basketball excellence was marked by his back-to-back Most Valuable Player (MVP) awards in 2019 and 2020. These years were not just about individual accolades but a reflection of his hard work, relentless improvement, and the undeniable impact he had on the court. In 2019, Giannis led the Milwaukee Bucks to the best record in the league, showcasing his all-around game by averaging 27.7 points, 12.5 rebounds, and 5.9 assists. His ability to dominate both ends of the floor, coupled with his leadership, made him a clear choice for the MVP award.

The 2020 season saw him elevate his game even further. Improving his statistical output to 29.5 points, 13.6 rebounds, and 5.6 assists per game, he became only the third player in NBA history to win both the MVP and Defensive Player of the Year (DPOY) awards in the same season, joining the elite company of Michael Jordan and Hakeem Olajuwon. This rare feat underscored his versatility and status as one of the game's most impactful players. The 2021 NBA season was perhaps the most defining chapter in his career. After years of playoff disappointments, the Milwaukee Bucks embarked on a post-season journey that would etch their names in basketball history.

Giannis's performance throughout the playoffs was nothing short of spectacular, but it was during the NBA Finals against the Phoenix Suns that he solidified his legacy. Overcoming a knee injury that had cast doubt on his participation, he put forth an effort for the ages. He averaged 35.2 points, 13.2 rebounds, and 5.0 assists per game in the Finals, including a 50-point masterpiece in the clinching Game 6 victory. This performance not only earned him the Finals MVP award but also delivered the Milwaukee Bucks their first NBA Championship in 50 years. His journey from the streets of Athens to NBA champion was a narrative of perseverance, a dream realized through unwavering determination and sheer will.

Giannis's impact extends beyond his on-court achievements. His commitment to the Milwaukee Bucks and the city itself has endeared him to fans and residents alike. In December 2020, he signed a supermax extension with the Bucks, committing his future to the team that took a chance on him in the draft. This decision was a testament to his loyalty and his desire to build a legacy in Milwaukee.

Off the court, Giannis is known for his charity and community engagement. From funding basketball courts in Greece to supporting local charities in Milwaukee, his efforts to give back to the communities that have shaped him are commendable. His story is also a beacon of hope for immigrants and underprivileged youth around the world, embodying the belief that hard work and dedication can overcome any obstacle.

As he continues to write his story, the peak years of his career so far serve as a foundation for what is still to come. With a championship under his belt, MVP awards, and a host of other accolades, the future is bright for Giannis Antetokounmpo. Yet, for Giannis, the journey is far from over. The pursuit of greatness never ends, and the desire to improve, to win more championships, and to solidify his legacy drives him forward

(Tikkanen, 2024)·

CAREER HIGHLIGHTS

- Giannis was selected with the 15th overall pick in the 2013 NBA Draft by the Milwaukee Bucks. His selection marked the beginning of a new era for the Bucks.
- Antetokounmpo has won multiple NBA Most Valuable Player (MVP) Awards, securing back-to-back honors in the 2018-2019 and 2019-2020 seasons. His blend of size, speed, and skill has made him nearly unstoppable on both ends of the court.
- Giannis led the Milwaukee Bucks to an NBA Championship in 2021, earning NBA Finals MVP honors for his outstanding performance throughout the series.
- In addition to his offensive prowess, Giannis has been recognized for his defensive capabilities, winning the NBA Defensive Player of the Year Award in 2020.

- Representing Greece, Giannis has competed in several international competitions, showcasing his talents on the global stage and further establishing his status as one of basketball's elite players.
- Giannis's unique skill set and physical gifts have challenged traditional basketball positions and roles, leading many to consider him a prototype for the future of the sport.

> I'm going to do whatever it takes for me and my team to be successful.
>
> GIANNIS ANTETOKOUNMPO

CHAPTER 9
DERRICK ROSE

HISTORY WAS MADE ONCE AGAIN IN THE NBA DURING THE 2010-2011 season when a 22-year-old superstar named Derrick Rose became the youngest player to win the MVP award. Winning this prestigious award at such a young age highlights the incredible skill and athleticism he possessed. Coming into the 2010-2011 season, Rose and his Chicago Bulls were quietly optimistic about the year ahead. Besides their young superstar, they had a strong core group of players and a new coach, Tom Thibodeau.

Rose's performance that year was nothing short of spectacular, averaging 25 points, 7.7 assists, and 4.1 rebounds, showing a rare blend of scoring ability, playmaking skills, and overall athleticism. His explosive speed, agility, and ability to finish at the rim made him a constant threat on offense.

The Bulls finished the season with a 62-20 record, securing the top spot in the Eastern Conference. During the playoff run, the Bulls performed impressively on their way to the Eastern Conference Finals, with Rose leading the way. Finally, they came up against the powerhouse that was the Miami Heat, consisting of one of the best big threes of all time, LeBron James, Chris Bosh, and Dwyane Wade. The Bulls won game one convincingly, but in the next four games, the Heat focused their defense on Rose and won the rest of the series. But hopes were still high in Chicago; they had found their next big superstar and aimed to improve the next season.

The following season was shortened to only 66 games due to a lockout. Despite this, Derrick Rose and the Chicago Bulls had another impressive run, finishing again with the best record in the Eastern Conference. This set the stage for another run in the playoffs, and hopes were high in Chicago. The first game of the playoffs was held in the United Centre, and the Bulls were in control, with a large lead with only minutes to play. Rose, still on the court, picked up the ball and made his trademark run to the basket.

As he planted his left foot to jump, he came to an immediate stop, wincing in pain. This devastating injury proved to be the end of the high-flying Derrick Rose we knew in Chicago, and the Bulls had lost one of their only bright stars since Michael Jordan. In the aftermath of the game, news came out that he had suffered a catastrophic ACL tear in his left knee. This injury not only ended his season but also marked the beginning of a difficult chapter in his career. The basketball world watched as the youngest MVP in NBA history struggled to reclaim his place on the court.

His road to recovery was both physically and mentally grueling. The process involved multiple surgeries, extensive rehabilitation, and the challenge of regaining his elite level of athleticism. Beyond the physical toll, the mental and emotional strain of the injuries was profound. He had to confront not only the physical pain but also the frustration, doubt, and the very real fear that his career might never be the same. However, it was during these trying times that Rose's character shone through. His work ethic, resilience, and unwavering determination became the cornerstone of his recovery.

His return to the court in the 2013-2014 season was highly anticipated, but the shadow of his previous injury loomed large. His comeback was cut short when he tore the meniscus in his right knee, requiring another surgery and ending his season early after just 10 games.

This pattern of injury and recovery became a recurring theme, casting doubt on his ability to return to his MVP form. Each attempt to return to the NBA's elite was met with another obstacle, another injury that required rehabilitation and time away from the game he loved.

Beyond the physical pain and the frustration of repeated surgeries was the mental battle he faced. The psychological impact of such injuries is profound, with the constant uncertainty and the fear of never being able to play at the highest level again. Rose's resilience was tested not just on the physical front but in maintaining the mental toughness required to face each setback with the determination to overcome it.

Despite the repeated injuries, his spirit remained unbroken. He began to adapt his style of play, transitioning from relying on his unparalleled athleticism to developing a more balanced game that focused on shooting, passing, and a strategic approach. This evolution was a testament to his determination to remain relevant in the NBA, despite the physical limitations imposed by his injuries.

Through each painful recovery process, Rose's resilience shone through. His repeated injuries could have easily ended the career of a lesser player, but he refused to be defined by his setbacks. Instead, he worked tirelessly to regain his place on the court, embodying the spirit of resilience and determination.

Even though Rose was never going to give up on himself, it didn't mean that others would do the same. For the Chicago Bulls franchise, the belief in him had faded, and they believed that his injury troubles would be something he could not overcome. News of the trade to the New York Knicks sent shockwaves through Rose's world, leaving him heartbroken. The Bulls were not just any team to him; they represented his hometown, his dreams, and the place where he had become the youngest MVP in league history. The trade was a stark reminder of the business side of basketball, a painful lesson that even the most beloved players could be moved in an instant. This moment was a huge loss, the end of an era that had defined much of his adult life.

The move to New York was just the beginning of his journey through the NBA as he searched for a new home where he could contribute and feel valued. After a brief time with the Knicks, Rose found himself navigating brief stints with several teams, including the Cleveland Cavaliers and the Minnesota Timberwolves. Each stop was an opportunity to prove his worth and to show that he could still play at a high level, despite the injuries and the setbacks that had derailed his career.

It was with the Timberwolves that Rose began to find his footing again, reuniting with coach Tom Thibodeau, who had coached him during his most successful years in Chicago.

He managed to put his setbacks aside and get back to what he does best: dominate on the basketball court. The standout moment in his return came in 2018, in a game that reminded the world of his incredible talent.

On a brisk evening in Minneapolis, the Target Center was buzzing with excitement, but no one could have predicted the historic performance they were about to witness from Derrick Rose. This was not just any game; it was a defining moment in his career, a powerful statement of resilience and determination that would forever etch this night in the history of the NBA. The Minnesota Timberwolves were set to face the Utah Jazz, a formidable opponent with one of the league's toughest defenses. Rose, who had faced more than his share of challenges, including devastating injuries and team changes, was not the primary focus of pre-game discussions. Yet, as the game commenced, it became clear that he was about to do something special.

As the game began, Rose immediately made his presence felt. He was aggressive, driving to the basket with the same explosive speed that had once made him the youngest MVP in NBA history. His first-quarter performance was a sign of what was to come, as he effortlessly sliced through the Jazz's defense, scoring in a variety of ways. The crowd roared with each basket, sensing the beginning of an extraordinary performance.

As the game progressed into the second and third quarters, Rose's confidence seemed to grow with each play. He was everywhere, hitting mid-range jumpers, converting acrobatic layups, and even stepping back to drain three-pointers. The Jazz's defense, one of the best in the league, had no answer for him. With every basket, the energy in the Target Center surged. Fans were on their feet, chanting his name, enjoying the vintage performance they were witnessing. It was as if he had turned back the clock, reminding everyone of his once-unquestioned dominance.

Entering the final quarter, Rose had already scored a staggering number of points, but he was far from done. With the game hanging in the balance, he took over, showcasing not just his scoring ability but also his leadership and determination. Each possession seemed critical, and he responded with unmatched intensity, scoring crucial baskets down the stretch.

The most memorable moment came in the dying minutes of the game. With the Timberwolves clinging to a narrow lead, he drove to the basket against a sea of defenders, absorbing contact and finishing a difficult layup while drawing the foul. The crowd erupted as Rose pumped his fists in triumph, a mix of joy and relief washing over him as he converted the free throw to complete the three-point play. As the final buzzer sounded, the Target Center exploded into celebration.

Rose had scored 50 points, the highest total of his career, leading the Timberwolves to a hard-fought victory over the

Jazz. Teammates and opponents alike congratulated him, recognizing the significance of his achievement. But it was the emotional scene post-game that captured the hearts of many; Rose, overcome with emotion, wept openly on the court. It was a raw, poignant moment that transcended sports, symbolizing his long, difficult journey back from the brink.

His 50-point game was more than just a remarkable statistical achievement; it was a testament to his unbreakable spirit. For one night, he silenced his doubters, reminding the world of his talent and resilience. The performance was a beacon of hope, not just for him but for anyone facing adversity. It demonstrated that with determination, perseverance, and faith, it is possible to overcome even the most daunting challenges.

The energy in the Target Center that night was electric. Fans and players alike shared in his triumph, a collective experience that would be remembered for years to come. It was a night where basketball was more than just a game; it was a story of redemption, a celebration of human spirit and perseverance.

Derrick Rose's career trajectory is a tale rich with lessons on resilience, perseverance, and the unyielding spirit to overcome adversity.

His journey from being the youngest MVP in NBA history to facing potentially career-ending injuries, and then to authoring a remarkable comeback, shows the essence of never giving up, regardless of how impossible the obstacles may seem. Rose's story is not just about basketball; it's a showcase of human resilience, making it a source of inspiration for young readers and indeed anyone facing their own battles (Rosenbach & Smith, 2019).

CAREER HIGHLIGHTS

- Rose played one year of college basketball for the Memphis Tigers, leading them to the national championship game during the 2007-2008 season.
- Rose was selected with the 1st overall pick in the 2008 NBA Draft by his hometown team, the Chicago Bulls.
- He won the NBA Rookie of the Year Award in 2009, immediately establishing himself as a standout player in the league.
- In 2011, at the age of 22, Rose became the youngest player in NBA history to be named MVP.
- Despite the setbacks, Rose has been known for his determined efforts to return to the court and regain his form, including productive stints with several teams like the New York Knicks, Cleveland Cavaliers, Minnesota Timberwolves, and Detroit Pistons.
- One of the most memorable moments in his career came on October 31, 2018, when he scored a career-high 50 points in a game while playing for the

Minnesota Timberwolves, showcasing his resilience and talent.

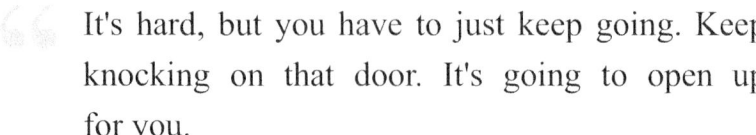 It's hard, but you have to just keep going. Keep knocking on that door. It's going to open up for you.

Derrick Rose

CHAPTER 10
BILL RUSSELL

For most young basketball athletes, the thought of winning one NBA championship would be the dream of a life-time. This win would represent a life of effort and sacrifice from both the player and their family. It would be the cherry on top of a journey that started in youth leagues, journeyed through high school, and eventually led to the NBA itself. But how about winning eleven championships? That would take an incredible athlete to do so, and only one man has been able to do it: the legendary Bill Russell.

In the heart of Monroe, Louisiana, in 1934, Bill Russell was born. His early life was far from easy. But from these humble beginnings, Russell would grow to change the game of basketball forever, becoming a beacon of inspiration for generations to come. His family moved to the West Coast in search of a better life when he was just eight years old. Oakland, California, became their new home, a place that offered new challenges and opportunities.

As a young boy, Bill was not immediately drawn to basketball. In fact, his first love was track and field. He excelled in high jumping, using his natural athleticism to soar to heights others could only dream of. It wasn't until a high school coach noticed his height and encouraged him to try out for the basketball team that his passion for the game began to grow.

High school was a turning point for Bill. Initially, he struggled with the sport. His early attempts at basketball were marked by awkwardness and a lack of skill. But he was not one to give up easily. With dedication, he practiced tirelessly, improving his skills, and learning the game. His hard work paid off when he led his high school team to back-to-back state championships, showcasing his emerging talent as a defensive powerhouse and rebounding phenom. Bill's high school success caught the attention of college scouts across the nation. However, it was the University of San Francisco (USF) that truly believed in his potential and offered him a scholarship, a decision that would alter the course of basketball history.

At USF, Bill Russell transformed from a promising player into a superstar. Under the guidance of Coach Phil Woolpert, he developed a unique style of play that focused on defense, teamwork, and an undying will to win. He led the USF Dons to an incredible 55 consecutive victories and two consecutive NCAA championships in 1955 and 1956. His impact on the court was revolutionary, introducing a level of athleticism and strategic defensive play that was previously unseen.

Bill arrived in the NBA on April 30, 1956, after being drafted by the St. Louis Hawks. However, his rights were soon traded to the Boston Celtics, a team hungry for success but lacking the final piece to clinch championship glory. Russell was that missing piece, but his journey was not without its hurdles. Adapting to the professional level, he faced off against more experienced and skilled opponents. However, his unmatched work ethic, coupled with his unique basketball IQ, allowed him to quickly climb the ranks, transforming challenges into stepping stones.

The 1957 NBA Championship, Russell's first, was a testament to his impact on the Celtics. Facing the St. Louis Hawks in a grueling seven-game series, his defensive masterclass in the decisive Game 7 was a spectacle of determination and skill. His rebounding and shot-blocking not only stopped the Hawks' offense but also inspired the Celtics, helping them to their first title.

This victory was not just a triumph but a statement of the Celtics' growing dynasty, with Russell as its leader.

The second championship in 1959 set the stage for what would become the most dominant run in NBA history. Russell, fresh off the taste of victory from his first championship, was hungry for more. This season, the Celtics swept the Minneapolis Lakers in the Finals, a feat that showcased not only his defensive mastery but also his evolving offensive game. It was a showing of dominance, a clear message to the league that the Celtics were not a one-hit wonder but a force to be reckoned with.

As our story continues, we see the Celtics' journey through the early 1960s, a period where Russell's rivalry with Wilt Chamberlain began to take center stage. Each championship added to the Celtics' legacy was a chapter in this rivalry, with Russell often emerging victorious, not solely through individual skill but by elevating his team to perform as a unit. The 1962 Finals against the Lakers, decided in a dramatic Game 7 overtime, shows this perfectly. His clutch performance under the highest pressure showcased his leadership and determination.

Fast forward to 1963 and 1964, where the Celtics, under Russell's guidance, continued their dominance. These years were marked by his unmatched defensive capabilities, which were the key to the Celtics' strategy.

His ability to alter the course of a game without scoring a point was revolutionary, changing how defense was perceived in the game of basketball. Our story would be incomplete without the 1966 championship, Russell's ninth. This title was particularly sweet, as it came against a backdrop of great personal and professional pressure. He, now also serving as the team's head coach, led the Celtics to victory against the Lakers, solidifying his legacy as one of the greatest leaders in sports history.

The sequence of championships from the first to the tenth is made of moments of brilliance, battles against formidable foes, and the relentless pursuit of excellence. Each title was a testament to Russell's leadership, both on and off the court. His ability to inspire his teammates, to demand the best from them and himself, and to navigate the highs and lows of a tough season is what set him apart.

Then came the magical night, where Bill and the Celtics won their 11th championship, in the 1968-69 NBA season. This chapter in basketball history is not just a tale of victory but a story of resilience, leadership, and an unbreakable spirit.

The 1968-69 season was Russell's last, his final act on the basketball stage, and it could not have been scripted any better.

By this time, Russell was not only the Celtics' defensive anchor but also their head coach, making him the first African

American to hold such a position in NBA history. This dual role underscored his contribution to the game and added another layer of significance to the Celtics' quest for another championship.

The road to the 1969 NBA Finals was anything but easy. The Celtics, no longer the dominant force of the early '60s, were seen as underdogs. Their journey through the playoffs was a testament to their grit, with Russell leading from the front, his knowledge as a coach as vital as his contributions on the court. The Celtics faced fierce competition, particularly from the Philadelphia 76ers and the New York Knicks, but Russell's leadership, both tactical and inspirational, guided them through.

The Finals pitted the Celtics against the Los Angeles Lakers, a team full of stars, including Jerry West, Elgin Baylor, and Wilt Chamberlain. The Lakers were favored to win, their roster a seemingly impossible obstacle for the aging Celtics. However, what unfolded over the course of this series is a story of determination, the power of experience, and the unbreakable spirit of Bill Russell.

Despite trailing in the series, the Celtics, under Russell's guidance, mounted a comeback that is etched in NBA history. His defensive skill, coupled with his strategic plays as coach, turned the tide in favor of the Celtics.

His matchup with Chamberlain in this series was symbolic of their long rivalry, with Bill using his intellect, defensive skills, and unparalleled understanding of the game to counteract Chamberlain's physical dominance. The series reached its climax in Game 7, held in the heart of Los Angeles. The Celtics, led by Russell, secured a narrow victory, clinching their eleventh championship in thirteen years. Russell's performance in this series, especially in the decisive game, was a fitting finale to his incredible career. His ability to elevate his game and lead his team under the most intense pressure solidified his legacy as one of the greatest winners in sports history.

Since that historic season, no player has come close to matching Russell's record of eleven NBA championships. This record stands as a testament to his longevity, resilience, and dominance in the sport. It is a benchmark of excellence that transcends generations, a symbol of what can be achieved through dedication, teamwork, and an unwavering commitment to success.

In closing, Bill Russell's eleventh NBA championship is more than a historical footnote. It is a shining beacon of achievement in the world of sports, a record that has stood the test of time. His legacy, characterized by this unparalleled feat, continues to inspire athletes and sports fans around the world. It serves as a reminder that greatness is not defined by talent alone but by the ability to unite others towards a common goal, to lead with integrity, and to face every challenge with courage and determination. Bill Russell's eleventh championship is a testament to a career marked by triumphs, a record of his status as one of the greatest athletes of all time—a record unbroken, a legacy unmatched (Shoals, 2024).

CAREER HIGHLIGHTS

- Russell played college basketball for the University of San Francisco, leading them to two consecutive NCAA championships in 1955 and 1956.
- Russell won 11 NBA championships with the Celtics, including a record eight consecutive titles from 1959 to 1966. This achievement makes him one of the most decorated athletes in North American sports history.
- He was named the NBA Most Valuable Player (MVP) five times (1958, 1961, 1962, 1963, and 1965).
- Russell is widely regarded as one of the greatest defenders and rebounders in basketball history, leading the NBA in rebounds four times during his career.
- In 1966, he became the first African American head coach in NBA history (and in any major sport in the United States), serving as a player-coach for the Celtics until his retirement in 1969.
- Russell's impact on the game was honored by the NBA when they renamed the NBA Finals MVP

Award the Bill Russell NBA Finals Most Valuable Player Award in 2009.

- Russell was inducted into the Naismith Memorial Basketball Hall of Fame in 1975 and was later inducted as a coach in 2021, making him one of only a few individuals to be enshrined as both a player and a coach.
- Before his professional career, Russell won a gold medal with the U.S. basketball team at the 1956 Melbourne Olympics.
- In 2011, President Barack Obama awarded Russell the Presidential Medal of Freedom, the nation's highest civilian award, in recognition of his accomplishments on the court and his contributions to the civil rights movement.

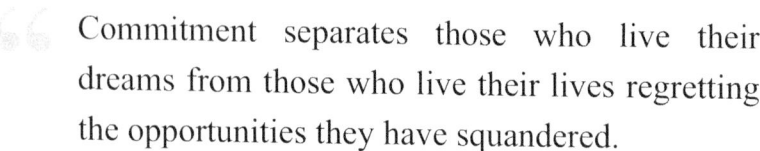 Commitment separates those who live their dreams from those who live their lives regretting the opportunities they have squandered.

BILL RUSSELL

CHAPTER 11
KOBE BRYANT

KOBE BRYANT'S FAREWELL GAME ON APRIL 13, 2016, WAS not just another basketball match; it was an event that celebrated the illustrious career of one of the greatest basketball players of all time. In a packed Staples Center in Los Angeles, fans, celebrities, and players from around the league gathered to witness the final act of the Black Mamba. The Los Angeles Lakers faced the Utah Jazz, and what unfolded was nothing short of a Hollywood script, with Kobe scoring 60 points, leading the Lakers to a 101-96 victory. This tale delves into the details of the game, its historic significance, and the incredible career of one of the greatest competitors of all time.

KOBE
BRYANT
"BLACK MAMBA"

From the opening tip, it was clear that this was Kobe's night. The Lakers fed him the ball on nearly every possession, and the crowd roared with every shot he took. Bryant started the game off slowly, his shots not falling with his usual precision, but as the game progressed, so did his performance. By half-time, he had scored 22 points, but the Lakers trailed the Jazz.

In the second half, Kobe found his rhythm. With every jumper, layup, and three-pointer, he edged closer to a scoring milestone that seemed unthinkable at the start of the night. The crowd grew louder, standing on their feet, chanting his name. Celebrities and former players were seen cheering and marveling at the spectacle. His teammates, fully aware of the magnitude of the moment, looked for him at every opportunity, wanting to ensure his career ended on a high note. As the fourth quarter wound down, Kobe became unstoppable. With just under two minutes left, he hit a go-ahead jumper to give the Lakers the lead. The arena erupted, sensing the historic nature of the moment. Then, with 31 seconds left, he was fouled and went to the free-throw line. He sank both shots, reaching 60 points. The Staples Center reached a fever pitch, celebrating not just the points but the end of an era.

Kobe's 60-point finale was more than just a remarkable athletic achievement; it was a symbolic passing of the torch, a farewell from one of the game's most iconic figures. It was the highest-scoring game for any player in his final game, a testament to his relentless work ethic and competitive spirit.

The game was a microcosm of his career: the struggle, the perseverance, and ultimately, the triumph. Let's now take a look back at one of the most iconic careers of all time, and understand why fans of basketball and sport in general will never forget the name Kobe Bryant.

Born on August 23, 1978, in Philadelphia, Pennsylvania, Kobe was the youngest of three children and the only son of Joe Bryant, a professional basketball player who had a notable career in the NBA and overseas. This environment filled Kobe with a passion for basketball from a very young age, setting the stage for his own basketball career.

From the moment he could walk, Kobe was surrounded by basketball. His early years were spent in Italy, where his father continued his professional career after leaving the NBA. It was here, in the Italian leagues, that Kobe first began to hone his skills against older, more experienced players. The international experience enriched his understanding of the game, as he absorbed diverse playing styles and tactics that would later define his versatile approach on the court.

The Bryant family returned to the United States in 1991, settling in the Philadelphia suburb of Lower Merion. It was at Lower Merion High School that Kobe's basketball career truly began to take flight. Even as a freshman, his talent was undeniable. Standing out for his work ethic as much as his skill, he quickly became the cornerstone of the Aces' basketball program.

Under the guidance of Coach Gregg Downer, Kobe trans-formed from a promising talent into a high school phenomenon. By his sophomore year, he was already recognized as one of the top players in the country. His game was characterized by an incredible scoring ability, a relentless work ethic, and a deep understanding of basketball strategy. His junior year saw him average over 30 points per game, leading Lower Merion to their first state championship in over fifty years.

His senior year was nothing short of spectacular. He averaged 30.8 points, 12 rebounds, 6.5 assists, 4 steals, and 3.8 blocks per game, showcasing his all-around talent and dominance on the court. His performances were electrifying, drawing crowds that included NBA scouts, celebrities, and basketball fans from across the nation. Kobe's high school career finished with a magical state championship run, solidifying his status as a national star. Off the court, he was named the Naismith High School Player of the Year, a fitting capstone to his high school career.

The transition from high school phenom to NBA rookie is a path fraught with challenges, expectations, and the relentless pressure to perform at the world's highest level of basketball competition. For Kobe, selected 13th overall by the Charlotte Hornets in the 1996 NBA Draft and then traded to the Los Angeles Lakers, this transition marked the beginning of an illustrious career that would forever alter the landscape of the NBA.

Kobe's entry into the NBA in the 1996-97 season was met with immense anticipation. At just 18 years old, he was the youngest player in NBA history at the time. His rookie season, under the guidance of then-Lakers coach Del Harris, was a mix of flashes of brilliance and the typical growing pains experienced by young players. He averaged 7.6 points, 1.9 rebounds, and 1.3 assists per game, respectable numbers for a rookie but just a glimpse of what was to come. Despite limited playing time, his work ethic, athleticism, and competitive fire were evident. He won the 1997 Slam Dunk Contest, heralding his arrival on the NBA stage and showcasing his incredible athleticism and charisma.

Kobe's development took a significant leap in his second season. His scoring average more than doubled, and his role on the team expanded under the Lakers' new head coach, Phil Jackson. The arrival of Jackson and the implementation of the triangle offense were pivotal in his career. This system allowed him to maximize his skills and begin to emerge as one of the premier talents in the league.

The 1999-2000 season marked a turning point for Kobe and the Lakers. Alongside Shaquille O'Neal, he formed one half of one of the most dominant duos in NBA history. His game reached new heights, as he averaged 22.5 points, 6.3 rebounds, and 4.9 assists per game.

The Lakers finished the season with a 67-15 record, and Kobe earned his first All-Star Game selection, an honor that would become a fixture of his career. The peak of Kobe's early NBA days came with the Lakers' three consecutive NBA championships from 2000 to 2002. During these championship runs, his role as a clutch performer and fearless competitor was solidified. In the 2000 NBA Finals against the Indiana Pacers, his performance in Game 4 was a defining moment. Despite suffering an ankle injury earlier in the series, Kobe stepped up in the absence of an injured O'Neal, scoring 28 points and leading the Lakers to a crucial overtime victory.

These early years set the stage for Kobe's evolution into a global icon. His relentless pursuit of greatness, combined with a skill set that seemed to have no bounds, made him a favorite among fans and a respected adversary among peers. His early NBA days were marked by his incredible work ethic, a characteristic that would define his entire career. He was notorious for his early morning and late-night workouts, constantly seeking to improve his game and push the boundaries of his physical and mental capabilities.

His early NBA career laid the foundation for what would become one of the most storied careers in sports history. His rise from a high school sensation to an NBA superstar was marked by relentless improvement, a competitive spirit, and a deep love for the game of basketball.

These early years were not just about personal accolades or the start of a championship dynasty; they were about the birth of a legend who would inspire countless individuals to strive for greatness in their own lives. The early 2000s witnessed the rapid ascent of Kobe into the area of basketball's all-time greats. This period, often referred to as Kobe's peak years, was characterized by extraordinary personal achievements, continued team success, and performances that will be remembered throughout NBA history. From the 2002-03 season through to the 2009-10 season, his brilliance on the basketball court was unmatched, showcasing his evolution from a talented youngster into a global sports icon.

Following the Lakers' three-peat from 2000 to 2002, Kobe entered a phase of his career where his individual talents truly shone. The 2005-06 and 2006-07 seasons were particularly emblematic of his dominance. During the 2005-06 season, he averaged a career-high 35.4 points per game, leading the league in scoring and cementing his status as one of the most potent offensive weapons in the game. It was during this season that Kobe scored 81 points against the Toronto Raptors, the second-highest single-game scoring performance in NBA history, showcasing his incredible scoring ability and relentless determination.

His peak years were not just about individual accolades; they were also a testament to his growth as a leader and his ability to adapt his game to lead his team to success.

The departure of Shaquille O'Neal in 2004 had marked a new era for the Lakers, with Kobe emerging as the undisputed leader of the team. His leadership was put to the test, and he responded by guiding the Lakers through periods of transition, including roster overhauls and changes in the coaching staff. The 2007-08 season marked a turning point for Kobe and the Lakers. The acquisition of Pau Gasol gave him the reliable second star he needed to propel the Lakers back to championship contention. That season, he was named the NBA's Most Valuable Player (MVP) for the first time in his career, a recognition of his all-around excellence and leadership on and off the court.

His peak years would not be complete without mentioning his return to the NBA Finals and the Lakers' resurgence as a championship dynasty. The Lakers reached the NBA Finals in three consecutive years from 2008 to 2010, winning back-to-back championships in 2009 and 2010. These victories were a testament to Kobe's relentless pursuit of excellence and his ability to elevate his game when it mattered most. In both championship runs, he was named the Finals MVP, further solidifying his legacy as one of the game's greatest clutch performers.

Kobe's career was characterized by breathtaking performances, unmatched work ethic, and a competitive fire that burned brighter than ever.

Off the court, Kobe's influence extended beyond basketball, as he became a cultural icon known around the world. His dedication to his craft, his ability to perform under pressure, and his commitment to winning left an indelible mark on the NBA and on sports fans globally. His career was not without challenges, including injuries and team dynamics, but Kobe's resilience and determination always shone through. His basketball genius, his strategic mind, and his physical prowess all combined to create a legacy that will be remembered for generations to come.

In reflecting on Kobe Bryant's life and career, we witness the journey of an athlete who transcended the sport to become a symbol of excellence and determination. Through his achievements, he inspired countless individuals to pursue their dreams with the same passion and commitment he demonstrated every time he stepped onto the basketball court. His story is not just a chapter in this book; it is a testament to the enduring legacy of one of the greatest to ever play the game of basketball (LakersNation.com, 2023)·

CAREER HIGHLIGHTS

- Kobe spent part of his childhood in Italy before returning to the U.S. He was drafted straight out of Lower Merion High School by the Charlotte Hornets with the 13th overall pick in the 1996 NBA Draft and was then traded to the Los Angeles Lakers, where he spent his entire 20-year career.

- Kobe won five NBA championships with the Lakers (2000-2002, 2009-2010), showcasing his leadership and skill in crucial moments.

- He was named the NBA Most Valuable Player (MVP) in 2008, recognizing his excellence during the regular season.

- Bryant was awarded the NBA Finals MVP twice (2009, 2010), further cementing his legacy as a clutch performer in the playoffs.

- Kobe won two NBA scoring titles (2006, 2007), highlighting his incredible offensive talent and ability to dominate games.

- One of his most memorable performances came on January 22, 2006, when he scored 81 points against the Toronto Raptors, the second-highest single-game scoring total in NBA history.

- Bryant represented the United States in the Olympics, winning gold medals in 2008 (Beijing) and 2012 (London).

- Kobe's work ethic, known as the "Mamba Mentality," has inspired countless athletes and fans worldwide, embodying dedication, resilience, and the relentless pursuit of greatness.

From the beginning, I wanted to be the best. I had a constant craving, a yearning, to improve and be the best.

KOBE BRYANT

CHAPTER 12
MAGIC AND LARRY

ONCE UPON A TIME, IN THE LAND OF BASKETBALL, TWO YOUNG stars were destined to light up the game's sky brighter than anyone had ever seen. This is the tale of Earvin "Magic" Johnson and Larry Bird, whose rivalry on the court formed a friendship that would inspire countless fans and players alike. Their story isn't just about basketball; it's a showcase of how competition can forge respect, and how adversaries can turn into allies.

EARVIN "MAGIC" JOHNSON

LARRY BIRD

"LARRY LEGEND"

In the late 1970s, the basketball world buzzed with excitement over two college players. On one side was Magic Johnson, an energetic young man with a magnetic smile and a playing style that seemed to defy reality. On the other side stood Larry Bird, a hardworking and fiercely competitive player with a sharp-shooting ability that could stun audiences. They were different in many ways: Magic hailed from the bustling city of Lansing, Michigan, while Larry grew up in the small town of French Lick, Indiana. Their paths to greatness seemed parallel but separate—until destiny brought these titans together.

The first clash occurred in college, during the 1979 NCAA Championship. Magic's Michigan State Spartans faced off against Larry's Indiana State Sycamores. The game was more than just a battle for the title; it was the beginning of a rivalry that would captivate the basketball world for decades. The Spartans emerged victorious, and Magic Johnson claimed the championship, but something else happened that day. As these two giants shook hands, a mutual respect was born, a silent acknowledgment of each other's talents and the start of a competition that would push them to their limits.

As fate would have it, Magic was drafted by the Los Angeles Lakers, and Larry by the Boston Celtics. These teams were arch-rivals, their fierce competition stretching back decades, adding fuel to the budding rivalry between them.

The basketball world watched in awe as these two legends transformed the NBA, their competition bringing out the best in each other and their teams. Their styles were as different as their backgrounds. Magic was a master of showmanship, his playmaking skills and infectious energy bringing a new level of excitement to the game. He could score, but his true magic lay in his ability to make his teammates better, his passes finding them in ways that seemed impossible. Larry, on the other hand, was a quiet force, his precision and work ethic making him one of the best shooters the game had ever seen. He was a true competitor, never backing down and always pushing himself harder.

Despite their rivalry, Magic and Larry shared many similarities. Both were leaders, driven by a deep love for the game and an undying desire to win. Their battles on the court were fierce, but off the court, a friendship began to form. They discovered that they were both just young athletes who loved basketball, each pushing the other to reach heights they might not have achieved alone.

The story of Magic Johnson and Larry Bird didn't end with their epic clash in college; it was just the beginning of a rivalry that would define an era in the NBA. As they stepped onto the professional stage, the stakes were higher, the lights brighter, and their rivalry became the heartbeat of basketball. Johnson's entrance into the NBA was nothing short of spectacular.

With a flair for the dramatic, he led the Los Angeles Lakers to an NBA Championship in his rookie year. It was a fairy-tale start to a career, capped off by Magic stepping in for the injured Kareem Abdul-Jabbar in Game 6 of the Finals and playing every position on the court. He dazzled with 42 points, 15 rebounds, and 7 assists, a performance for the ages, and set the stage for the rivalry with Bird to flourish.

Meanwhile, Larry Bird was making his own mark with the Boston Celtics. Bird's rookie season was a testament to his work ethic and talent. He transformed the Celtics, a team that had won just 29 games the previous year, into a title contender. Bird's impact was immediate, his dedication to the game evident in every pass, every shot, and every minute he played. The stage was set for these two titans to dominate the league and etch their rivalry in the minds of fans everywhere.

The early 1980s were a time of renewal in the NBA, with the two young superstars leading the charge. The Lakers and Celtics quickly became the teams to beat, their every meeting an instant classic. Their games were more than just basketball; they were battles of tactics, style, and will. Magic, with his Showtime Lakers, played a fast-paced, electric style of basketball, a symphony of fast breaks and no-look passes. Bird, on the other hand, represented the blue-collar, gritty basketball of the Celtics, a blend of incredible shooting, tough defense, and unselfish play.

Their individual accolades began to pile up. Magic was named MVP three times in the 1980s, while Bird won three consecutive MVP awards from 1984 to 1986, a feat only matched by the legendary Bill Russell and the incomparable Wilt Chamberlain. Yet, it was their head-to-head matchups that excited fans, each game a chapter in the ongoing rivalry.

The 1984 NBA Finals was their first clash on basketball's biggest stage, a grueling seven-game series that pushed both men to their limits. The Celtics emerged victorious, but the respect between Magic and Larry grew stronger. They pushed each other to excel, to dig deeper, and to reach heights they hadn't known were possible. Magic's response to the loss was to come back stronger, leading the Lakers to an NBA Championship the following year and claiming the Finals MVP. The message was clear: every setback was an opportunity to come back stronger.

Off the court, their relationship evolved. They appeared together in commercials, breaking down barriers and showcasing their growing friendship to the world. In 1985, they jointly won the NBA's first-ever co-MVPs of the All-Star Game, a fitting tribute to their shared dominance of the league. Yet, on the court, their battles remained fierce, a testament to their competitive spirit and unyielding desire to win.

The 1980s saw Magic and Larry lead their teams to eight NBA Championships between them, reigniting the Lakers-Celtics rivalry and bringing the NBA to new levels of popularity.

The late 1980s marked the peak of their rivalry, as age and injuries began to take their toll. However, their impact on the game and on each other's lives remained. They had pushed each other to heights they might not have reached on their own, setting new standards of excellence and re-writing what it meant to be competitors and champions.

As the sun set on the careers of Earvin "Magic" Johnson and Larry Bird, their rivalry transitioned from the hardcourt battles of the 1980s into NBA history, leaving a permanent mark on the sport of basketball and on the hearts of fans worldwide. This concluding chapter celebrates their legendary competition, their profound impact on the game, and the deep respect and friendship that flourished between two of basketball's greatest icons.

Magic and Larry entered the NBA at a time when the league was in desperate need of new talent. Their rivalry became the lifeline of the NBA, injecting excitement, class, and a new level of competitiveness into the game.

Through their epic showdowns, they not only elevated their teams to new heights but also continued one of the most storied rivalries in sports history. Their battles were more than games; they were captivating narratives that turned basketball into a global spectacle. Their impact on the sport can be measured in various ways: increased viewership, sold-out arenas, and a significant rise in NBA merchandise sales.

However, their true legacy lies in the way they changed the game. Magic, with his magnetic personality and unparalleled court vision, transformed the point guard position, showing that an almost 6'9" player could lead a team with finesse and imagination. Bird, with his relentless work ethic and sharp shooting, redefined what it meant to be a forward, combining the toughness of a power player with the shooting accuracy of a guard. Together, they inspired a generation of players to think differently about their roles and capabilities on the basketball court.

Beyond their on-court achievements, Magic and Larry played pivotal roles in bridging the gap between the NBA and its fans. Their rivalry was accessible and relatable, embodying the competitive spirit that is at the heart of sports. They showed that rivalry doesn't have to breed hatred; instead, it can foster respect and admiration. The way they spoke of each other, not just as competitors but as friends and as people they admired, taught fans and young players alike the value of sportsmanship.

Their respect for each other was always evident. Magic once said, "Larry, you only told me one lie. You said there will be another Larry Bird. Larry, there will never, ever, ever be another Larry Bird." Meanwhile, Bird expressed his admiration for Magic, saying, "Magic is head and shoulders above everybody else. I've always said that, and I still say it."

Their mutual respect and admiration transcended their rivalry, highlighting the essence of true sportsmanship.

The legacy of Magic Johnson and Larry Bird is not solely defined by their championships, MVP awards, or All-Star appearances. It is also shown in the countless driveways, playgrounds, and gyms around the world where young players copy their moves, dreaming of achieving greatness. It lives on in the spirit of competition and friendship that defines the best of sports. Their story is a reminder that while the game may end, the lessons, and memories forged through competition last a lifetime (Merlino, 2017).

CAREER HIGHLIGHTS MAGIC

- Magic rose to prominence playing for Michigan State University, leading the Spartans to the NCAA championship in 1979.
- Johnson was selected 1st overall by the Los Angeles Lakers in the 1979 NBA Draft.
- Magic led the Lakers to five NBA championships during the 1980s (1980, 1982, 1985, 1987, 1988), playing a central role in one of the most dominant teams in league history.
- Johnson was named the NBA Most Valuable Player (MVP) three times (1987, 1989, 1990), reflecting his dominance and all-around contributions to his team.

- He won the NBA Finals MVP award three times (1980, 1982, 1987), including an extraordinary performance in his rookie season where he started as center in place of the injured Kareem Abdul-Jabbar in Game 6 of the 1980 NBA Finals.
- Johnson led the NBA in assists four times, showcasing his extraordinary vision and playmaking ability.
- He was a member of the original "Dream Team," winning an Olympic gold medal with the United States basketball team in the 1992 Barcelona Olympics.
- Magic was inducted into the Naismith Memorial Basketball Hall of Fame in 2002, cementing his legacy as one of the game's all-time greats.

Ask not what your teammates can do for you. Ask what you can do for your teammates.

MAGIC JOHNSON

CAREER HIGHLIGHTS LARRY

- Bird was selected by the Boston Celtics with the 6th overall pick in the 1978 NBA Draft, joining the team for the 1979-1980 season.

- Bird led the Celtics to three NBA championships (1981, 1984, 1986), showcasing his leadership and versatility on the court.
- He was named the NBA Most Valuable Player (MVP) three consecutive times (1984, 1985, 1986), becoming the first forward to win three MVP awards in a row.
- Bird won the NBA Finals MVP award twice (1984, 1986) for his outstanding performances in the championship series.
- Known for his scoring ability, Bird won the NBA scoring title in the 1983-1984 season and was also a proficient rebounder and passer, making him one of the most versatile players in the league.
- Bird won the NBA's first three three-point shooting contests at All-Star Weekend, showcasing his sharpshooting skills. He also led the league in free-throw percentage four times.
- Bird was a member of the original "Dream Team," winning an Olympic gold medal with the United States basketball team in the 1992 Barcelona Olympics, despite playing with a severe back injury.
- Larry Bird was inducted into the Naismith Memorial Basketball Hall of Fame in 1998, solidifying his legacy as one of the game's all-time greats.
- After retiring from playing, Bird had successful stints as a coach and executive, winning NBA Coach of the

Year in 1998 with the Indiana Pacers and NBA Executive of the Year in 2012.

I wasn't real quick, and I wasn't real strong. Some guys will just take off and it's like, whoa. So I beat them with my mind and my fundamentals.

Larry Bird

CONCLUSION

As our journey through the heart-stopping, awe-inspiring world of basketball comes to a close, I hope that the stories you've found within these pages have lit a spark within you. Each story was a beacon of what it means to strive, to fail, and yet, to rise again stronger than ever. These athletes, with their remarkable journeys, have not only redefined the game but have shown us that the spirit of basketball goes far beyond the court.

I wrote this book with a hope—a hope that by sharing these stories, more young hearts would be inspired to pick up a basketball, to feel the joy of playing, to experience the cama-raderie of a team, and to learn the valuable life lessons that only sports can teach.

Whether you dream of playing professionally or simply enjoy shooting hoops in your backyard, remember that every dribble, every shot, and every game is a step toward becoming the best version of yourself.

As we part ways, I encourage you not to let this be the end of your journey with basketball. Let it be just the beginning. Get out there and play, practice, be a part of a team, make your own stories, and maybe, inspire others just as you have been inspired. Remember, the greatest stories are not just told; they are made.

In closing, I thank you for sharing this journey with me. May the lessons you've learned, the stories you've read, and the legends you've met inspire you to chase your dreams, on and off the court. Here's to your journey, to your dreams, and to the countless games ahead. May your love for basketball grow stronger with every game you play, every shot you take, and every challenge you overcome.

A MESSAGE FROM US

How would you like to play your part in helping the next generation of athletes get on the court?

AUTHOR

When I was a kid, I loved watching sports with my family every weekend. This made me want to play sports too, and it led me to some amazing adventures.

Playing sports taught me a lot. I became more confident, made great friends, and learned how to be part of a team. I even got to travel the world because of sports, all thanks to those days watching games with my family.

I wrote this book to share my love for sports with kids everywhere and to encourage them to play and enjoy sports too. But

I need your help to do this. To help this book reach more kids, I need you to support it.

If this book has inspired you, please consider spending just 30 seconds to leave a review on Amazon. Your feedback can help other young sports enthusiasts discover this book and, hopefully, ignite a new passion in them.

Here's how to leave a review:

1. Go to the "Returns & Orders" section at the top right corner of Amazon.
2. Find my book, click "Write a product review," and tell us what you think.

Thank you from the bottom of my heart :)

BIBLIOGRAPHY

1. *Bogues, Tyrone "Muggsy" | Encyclopedia.com.* (n.d.).
2. Shoals, B. (2024, February 8). *Bill Russell | Biography, Height, Championships, & Facts.* Encyclopedia Britannica.
3. Biography.com Editors. (2024, February 22). Stephen Curry. *Biography.*
4. Rosenbach, D., & Smith, S. A. (2019). *I'll show you.* Triumph Books (IL).
5. Geoffreys, C. (2014). *Allen Iverson: the Inspiring Story of One of Basketball's Greatest Shooting Guards.*
6. Chin, D. (2022, February 4). The Legacy of Linsanity, 10 years later. *The Ringer.*
7. Tikkanen, A. (2024, March 9). *Giannis Antetokounmpo | Height, Brothers, Stats, & Milwaukee Bucks.* Encyclopedia Britannica.
8. Geoffreys, C. (2016). *Dirk Nowitzki: the Inspiring Story of One of Basketball's Best European Stars.*
9. The Editors of Encyclopaedia Britannica. (n.d.). *LeBron James summary.* Encyclopedia Britannica.
10. LakersNation.com. (2023, February 24). *Kobe Bryant Biography | Early Life, Career & Stats | Lakers Nation.* Lakers Nation.
11. Piccotti, T. (2024, February 22). Michael Jordan. *Biography.*
12. Merlino, D. (2017, October 3). Magic Johnson and Larry Bird: the rivalry that transformed the NBA. *Bleacher Report.*